The First Year of Forever is a deeply moving, clear-eyed account of a couple's first year of bereavement following their son's death: what they lost, what they gained, how they survived.

Nothing in life prepares you for the loss of a child. Late one night, Ben Van Vechten woke to discover their seventeen-year-old son, Peter, had not come home yet. When they called the police, they heard the worst. There'd been an accident. Their son had hit a telephone pole. Peter was dead.

The First Year of Forever is the story of their first year after that death: the shock and slow recovery; the day-to-day details of living; the sorrow and anger and what it took to work them out; the process of pulling their life together, with the help of family, friends and a bereaved parents' group called Compassionate Friends.

Through the very ordinariness of the death and of the life before — an often stormy adolescent-parent relationship — a story emerges of enormous benefit for anyone who has lost someone close. The events, thoughts and feelings of that first year stand as both a comfort and a guidepost. "We have suffered," writes Ben Van Vechten, "but we have survived; we are hurting, but we are enduring." We endure, and feel, and learn with them.

Jacket design copyright © 1982 by Muriel Nasser

Photograph by Suzanne Van Vechten

THE FIRST YEAR OF FOREVER

THE FIRST YEAR OF FOREVER

Surviving the Death of Our Son

B. D. VAN VECHTEN

DWIGHT PUBLISHING

MENTOR, OHIO

1987

Library of Congress Cataloging in Publication Data

Van Vechten, B. D.
    The first year of forever.

        1. Death.   2. Van Vechten, B. D.   3. Van Vechten,
Suzanne.   4. Van Vechten, Peter.   I. Title.
BD444.V3   1982   155.9'37   82-45171
ISBN 0-689-11317-X   AACR2

Composition by American–Stratford Graphic Services, Inc.,
Brattleboro, Vermont
Manufactured by Dwight Publishing, Mentor, Ohio
Designed by Harry Ford
Second Printing

For Peter, of course

Death stalked the olive trees
Picking his men
His leaden finger beckoned
Again and again

JOHN LEPPER

In this sad world of ours, sorrow comes to all, and it often comes with bitter agony. Perfect relief is not possible except with time. You cannot now believe that you will ever feel better. But this is not true. You are sure to be happy again. Knowing this, truly believing it, will make you less miserable now. I have had enough experience to make this statement.

Attributed to ABRAHAM LINCOLN

ACKNOWLEDGMENTS

To:

Suzanne who relived in distressing detail the events and feelings of those dreadful days in order to make this book what it is;

my friends at Compassionate Friends, especially Bob Watts, who encouraged and supported me throughout this endeavor—including those who shared a few of the early chapters with me in a grubby hotel room in Baltimore;

and Jane and Michael Stern who suggested the idea in the first place

my everlasting gratitude

INTRODUCTION

MOST OF US do not deal well with death. The reasons are many and complex, of course, but certainly one reason is that we are, as Elisabeth Kübler-Ross and others have stated, a death-denying society. Despite the daily headlines of plane and car crashes, random violence, deadly fires, and so on, we are not very good at accepting the actuality of death. Death on television or in newspapers lacks reality. It is too removed, too distanced. In fact, there is nothing more absolute and final, nor anything more threatening to the self, than death. Another person's death brings home to us our own mortality.

Much in our society encourages us to deny death. Most dying takes place in hospitals, and most of us are not present at the moment of death of a loved one or friend. Additionally, hospitals are, oddly enough, poorly equipped to deal with the emotional impact of death. It is common knowledge now that many doctors and nurses cannot handle death because on some level the death of a patient represents their failure. Modern medicine is supposed to keep people alive.

There has been a steady movement over the past twenty to thirty years to consign the elderly to convalescent homes, nursing homes, and retirement communities. Too often today, the young grow up with little contact with the elderly on an intimate, daily basis. Those closest to death or in the process of dying are removed from our presence, to be seen only occasionally. Their deaths are almost abstract to us.

There has also been a movement recently to ignore the traditional forms of grieving. The rituals associated with death developed over the ages are considered too old fashioned or too primitive for our modern, sophisticated society. We do not stop to consider why these rituals evolved in the first place. Seldom do we see people wearing black clothing or even black armbands. Fewer and fewer people observe a mourning period and all that that entails. Often, the deceased are not laid out for viewing, or, if they are, only for those members of the immediate family. Further, this is virtually always done in funeral homes, and not, as it was years ago, at home. Many of us have grown up without ever seeing a dead person.

Usually, the details and arrangements following death are handled by just one member of the family, or, as is often the case, by a close friend of the family. Consequently, those closest to the deceased do little except sit around with their grief, "spared" the unpleasantness of dealing with the details of a loved one's death. We move from funeral home to church service to cemetery like automatons. A whole generation has grown up with an intellectual perception of death (sure, we all die) but not an emotional understanding of it.

When our only son, Peter, died, my wife and I, following the advice of a dear friend, as well as our own instincts, decided that we would actively involve ourselves in all aspects of the death proceedings and face as fully as we could the fact of his death. We realized that we would need all the aid and support we could get—from relatives, friends, professionals, anyone who cared and wanted to help. We recognized that our problem was twofold: getting through the next few days and getting through the rest of our lives. We were soon engulfed with an outpouring of sympathy, caring, and love. In turn, we quickly realized that reaching out to others was of enormous benefit to us.

We have lost our son (technically, my stepson) and he is irreplaceable, but we have gained other things. We have lost something that can never be restored; we have gained something that can never be lost. I feel both are worth discussing. This, then, is the story of our son's death and our first year of bereavement.

THE FIRST YEAR OF FOREVER

PROLOGUE

I WOKE UP at twenty-five minutes to four in the morning.
I noticed the hall light coming through a crack under our
bedroom door. A bad sign. I lay still for a few moments,
hoping sleep would return and spare my having to deal
with the worrisome problem of why the hall light was on
at this time of night. Sleep didn't come. I listened for the
sound of the television downstairs—a signal that Peter
had probably fallen asleep watching some late movie.
There was no sound. Anxiety pushed me out of bed.

As I walked across the small hallway separating our
bedrooms, I noticed a light on downstairs as well. I
checked Peter's room. He was not there. I went downstairs quietly, hoping not to wake my wife, Suzanne. He
was not there either. Remembering that he had bought a
moped the day before at the gas station where he was
working that summer, I went out to the garage. There
was no sign of the moped. Anxiety was turning into fear.

I went back into the house, wondering what to do.
Once before, when he was sixteen, Peter had failed to
come home. We had tracked him down the next day,

sleeping off his first drunk at a friend's house. Relief at finding him safe had replaced anger and recriminations. We had a long talk, stressing his responsibilities to us. We made it clear that, although we disapproved of his actions, the important points were his safety and our knowing where he was. He seemed to understand and agreed never to pull a stunt like that again. He was pretty good about following through on agreements, so I was all the more worried. How could he do this again? I felt anger rising.

Still uncertain what to do, I went upstairs to our bedroom. As I entered, Suzanne asked, "What's the matter?"

"Peter's not here," I said.

"What time is it?" she asked, her voice flat.

"A quarter of four," I answered. "The moped is gone."

We looked at each other a moment, our faces reflecting the exasperation, even the sense of betrayal, we felt at his having done it again. Our anger masked our fear. We discussed what to do. I told her I had heard him come in just after I had gone to bed about eleven-thirty. He had come upstairs and had then gone down again. Nothing unusual in that. Probably he was getting a snack and watching television. I had gone to sleep. Had I heard the soft sputtering of the moped engine as I drifted off? Sometimes I think I did.

We knew whom he had been with earlier in the evening. One of his friends was celebrating a birthday, and there had been a small get-together. Should we wait until seven to call so as not to disturb people? That's what we had done last time. It's not very pleasant waking people in the middle of the night. It's also not very pleasant having to ask people if they know where your son is. Suzanne forced the issue: this time we were not going to suffer the anxiety we had suffered before. We would find out where he was. After all, she argued, would we be upset if someone called us in the small hours looking for her child? Certainly not.

Since it was Suzanne's idea (or, at least, since she had voiced the idea), I gladly let her make the calls. No help at Coral's house; she had last seen Peter about eleven, just before he came home. Better luck at Greg's; Peter had been swimming with him at the reservoir. They had met there after the party and Peter had left about three o'clock, heading for home on his moped. Peter had been fine when Greg last saw him, no drinking or smoking. Greg sounded genuinely confused and concerned. That explained most of the missing time, but where the hell was he now? Did he have an accident? That idea had been sitting between us for some time, unspoken. Perhaps the moped had broken down? We considered my driving around the area, but as we live in a hybrid community—part rural, part suburb, with lots of back roads—we decided that would be a waste of time. The next call was obvious, but we were reluctant to make it. The tension was becoming almost painful.

I called the police and asked if they had any reports of accidents involving a teenager and a moped. Without answering my question, the cop asked my name. This didn't surprise me, for I figured it was probably standard procedure. He then asked my address. I think he may have asked another question or two; I just don't remember. My energies were devoted to keeping control of myself, to keeping calm. I was conscious of my heart thumping in my chest. I was also conscious that he still had not answered my question. It seemed as though I were on the phone for nearly thirty minutes; actually, it was probably closer to three. I know that he pinned down precisely where we lived. Finally he said, "There has been an accident just up the road from you. Near Kent Road. I think you should go up there immediately." The brief remainder of our conversation is vague in my mind. I asked if it was our son, but he said they had no name. I don't recall if I asked for other details or not. I probably was too frightened to. I do know that I didn't get any, and I have the sense that he may have repeated that I should leave at once.

Suzanne had gotten back into bed and pulled up the covers—no hiding the fear now; it was out in the open, and the frightened animal had retreated to its snug lair for protection. I told her what the cop had said. I started getting dressed and asked if she were going to come. With what seemed appropriate logic, she said she had better stay in case the phone rang. Within a minute or two I was leaving the house. I have little recollection of what was going through my mind as I drove out the driveway. Probably a repeated denial that it could be Peter. I was in a state of controlled panic. When I reached the crest of a small hill on our road, I saw the flashing light of two police cars no more than three hundred yards from our house. I pulled up behind one of the cars and got out. There were several cops and a civilian milling about. I had never been so alert, so aware of my surroundings.

One of the cops approached me. I told him that the officer at the police station had advised me to come to the scene of the accident. He asked if my son had been riding a moped. As we were talking, I became aware of a moped on the side of the road. He led me over to it. I was also aware of a bundled shape near a telephone pole about ten yards farther up the road. He shone his flashlight on the moped. I concentrated on it. It was the right color. Also, the front tire guard was missing; Peter had removed it earlier that day. I said it looked like my son's. It didn't look terribly damaged.

As we turned away, I searched desperately for explanations. Someone had stolen his moped, I decided. But that was unlikely. Then I had a better idea. Peter had loaned it to one of his friends. That was it! My momentary exhilaration was undercut by the realization of the suffering this would bring to whosever family it was. By this point we had reached the shape on the other side of the telephone pole. There was a tarpaulinlike covering over it. One of the other cops joined us.

"We'll have to ask you to make an identification," one of them said softly to me.

"Just give me a moment, please," I requested.

I was trying to get control of my breathing. Of all the stupid things, I thought, why can't I breathe properly? I couldn't seem to get enough oxygen into my lungs. My head felt light. I remember exhorting myself, "Don't be an ass; don't faint; hang tough."

The cop was explaining that they thought the moped with its relatively narrow tires had been thrown off course by the grating over a storm drain. This in turn had pushed the machine close enough to a piece of cement curbing so that the pedal hit it. At this point the moped flipped, throwing its driver head first into the telephone pole.

7

One of the cops was standing beside me; the other was kneeling by the covered form. He was looking up at me. I nodded to him. He pulled the cover away.

I stood for a while, my eyes riveted on the body, photographing the details with an awful, terrible clarity. I walked a few paces into the road, muttering, "Oh, sweet Jesus!" A wave of absolute rage broke over me, and I heard a series of "Fuck"s! exploding from my mouth. Everyone else was silent. I suddenly discovered I was on one knee in the middle of the road, my hand on the pavement to keep my balance. I had a powerful sense of self-consciousness, as if I were standing aside observing myself and the scene. Things seemed to be happening in slow motion. I felt the cop's arm around my shoulder. He asked me if I was all right. He seemed like a nice guy.

I stood up and walked back to the side of the road. I recognized the Grateful Dead T-shirt; the blue-jean jacket; the long, curly brown hair, now matted with blood. I recognized the half-opened brown eyes, now sightless, lifeless. I recognized the broken body. It was my son.

Peter was dead. He was seventeen.

CHAPTER

I

NOTHING IN LIFE prepared me for the loss of my own child. I sometimes had dreadful fantasies in which I imagined Peter dead. As painful as that experience was, it did not come close to the soul-crunching shock of the real thing. No one's death is really acceptable to us, although in the case of the senile or the painfully, terminally ill it can be a welcome release from the suffering of all those involved. We expect our parents to die. We grieve for them, of course, but their deaths don't shake our faith in the fundamental set of beliefs each of us holds, be they philosophical or religious. Any loved one's death reminds us of our mortality, but it does not necessarily disturb our sense of an ordered universe. This is not so with the death of a child.

We sense that something is intrinsically wrong. We are struck dumb by an overwhelming sense of unfairness. I know I was. Naturally, I was in a state of shock, although

I didn't realize it at the time. As I drove home from the scene of the accident, all I could think of was that he's dead and it makes no sense. (It is now over a year later and I still cannot get the fact that he is dead and it makes no sense.)

I shouldn't say that was all I could think of. I was also thinking of his mother waiting for me to return, waiting for me to say that Peter was okay—injured, perhaps, but okay. I knew from past experience that there was no point in trying to break news of this sort in a gentle, gradual way—better to just lay it on the line. Still, I'd been searching for the right words, instinctively trying to lessen the impact of the blow, to make it easier on Suzanne. I was also terrified that I wouldn't be able to get the words out. Some years ago when a close personal friend had died, I'd had to tell a mutual friend. It had taken several minutes because I simply couldn't speak. I'd open my mouth, but nothing would come. I kept clearing my throat, which had completely dried up, and shaking my head. I was able to tell Don that I had bad news for him and that I knew he would want to tell his wife personally, so that was why I'd caught him at the station before he went to work. But it took a lot of throat-clearing before I could say, "Frank is dead." I despised myself for putting Don through hell and for my own weakness. I felt like a character in a melodrama who cannot speak the necessary words because of an overdeveloped sensibility. God, I couldn't let that happen now.

Suzanne was standing in the living room and turned to face me as I walked in. I still had no idea what I would say. I could sense the tension; she was wound tight. Our eyes were fastened on each other as I walked toward her.

"Well, it's all over, Lovey," I said, shaking my head. "We'll never have to worry about him again."

She made some sort of noise and we held each other. We just stood there, not speaking, not even crying, just holding each other.

Finally, I said, "I want to go wait with him until the ambulance comes. Will you be all right here?"

Suzanne nodded. Neither of us questioned her remaining at home. At this point we were both playing the game of Protect the Mother From Harsh Realities, a game we soon abandoned. And a good thing we did, for one of Suzanne's bitterest regrets is that she did not go to Peter on the roadside.

"If you start to get upset, take the flashlight and walk up the road. I'll see it and come to you," I told her.

The ambulance arrived almost as soon as I did. They placed Peter in it. A line from *Hamlet* was running through my head, "I'll lug the guts into the neighbor room." Hamlet says this in a moment of severe agitation, a mixture of anger and cynicism, after he has killed Polonius. That's it, I thought. That's how I'll handle it—be tough-minded and cynical. Christ!

It had come down to this: all the loving and hating, all the caring and fighting, all the helping and hindering, all the hoping and fearing had brought me to this lonely country road a little after four on a muggy July morning to view the broken body of my dead son. This shouldn't be happening, I thought, as I got back into my car. How am I going to deal with this? How is Suzanne going to deal with this? How are we going to deal with this? Why has this happened? Christ!

The cop who was still there said they were taking Peter

to the hospital, where an autopsy would be performed. Whatever funeral home we contacted would then make the necessary arrangements.

I had no consistent pattern of thoughts; I doubt that I was "thinking" in the conventional sense of the word. I simply had an overwhelming sense of disbelief. When I got home, I noticed that Suzanne had kept busy while I was gone. The kitchen was straightened, the dishes from dinner put away, and the toaster thoroughly cleaned. In fact, the toaster was shining. Suzanne told me later that after I had left the first time she had gotten dressed and paced back and forth in the living room, her mind a muddle, simply waiting for my return. She had not yet realized that if Peter were only injured, the police would probably have told me to go to Norwalk Hospital rather than the scene of the accident. After I left the second time, she felt that need to be physically busy.

I described the accident to Suzanne, and, while I may have downplayed the gore a bit, I said the injuries appeared to have been fairly massive. "He couldn't have suffered, Lovey," I told her. "He must have died at once. Even the cops said so."

Most of me believed it, enough so that I said the words with conviction. But I think we both were just this side of complete certainty. I knew I was, I also knew that I would soon have to find out definitely, for my own peace of mind.

"I want my sister here, and we have to call Big Peter," Suzanne said. Sally and her husband, Gardiner, lived in Stamford, about twenty minutes away. Gardiner is the headmaster at King School where I teach. "Big Peter" is the appellation we used for Suzanne's first husband in order to avoid confusion between the two Peters. Suzanne and Big Peter had been divorced when Peter was two, and we had married when he was a little over three. He seemed to adjust well to having two fathers.

I pointed out to Suzanne that it was not yet four-thirty. Perhaps it was too early to disturb people. She looked at me as if I were crazy. I made the call to Sally and Gardiner.

Gardiner answered. I told him that I had some bad news. Peter had been killed in an accident. I added a few details and said that Suzanne wanted Sally. Gardiner would break the news to Sally, and they would be up shortly.

Suzanne then called Big Peter. He said he would go directly to his parents (he lives and works in New York, and his parents lived in Old Greenwich) and call us back from there.

"How did he sound?" I asked when she hung up. I was worried that he might blame us. We had always gotten along well (the divorce had been quite civilized) and always conferred about major decisions concerning Peter. Although we were in basic agreement about child rearing, Suzanne and I knew that he was not always happy with the way we put theory into practice—neither were we for that matter. However, things were going to be tough enough without accusations flying about. I knew that if I were in his place, I would want to know what the hell my son was doing tooling about the countryside at three o'clock in the morning.

Suzanne said there was no indication that he was

blaming us. Somehow that didn't make me feel any better. I guess I didn't need anyone else for imputations to fly around in my head.

We decided that we had better do some cleaning, as there would undoubtedly be a lot of people in and out of the house over the next few days. Suzanne dusted and straightened while I vacuumed. We didn't speak much; each of us seemed to be seeking comfort in furious physical activity. She even cleaned the top of the refrigerator—a necessary but seldom performed task. A shelf where we kept our cookbooks and some canisters also came under attack. The kitchen was glistening by the time Suzanne was through with it. After we finished downstairs, Suzanne said she wanted to shape up the pigsty, an irreverent but not wholly inaccurate description of Peter's room.

Peter had a large room divided by a partition that ran about three-quarters of its length. One half was used as a bedroom, the other as a sitting room. The furniture consisted of items he'd had since early childhood, a couple of bookcases I had made him, and a few pieces either given or appropriated over the years. The walls were completely covered with rock posters, athletic awards, and centerfolds. Part of the room divider was pegboard, from which hung some Civil War swords, a few World War II souvenirs of my father's, and various 1960s antiwar buttons. Virtually every surface in the room was cluttered with knickknacks, or junk, depending on one's point of view. Additionally, the room had a peculiar odor. Various colognes and after-shave lotions and a mild incense of some sort undoubtedly contributed, but to this day I don't know what else went into making his room smell as it did. It was by no means unpleasant, simply unusual. It was also distinctly Peter.

His room was an absolute mess. Articles of clothing in varying degrees of dirtiness were strewn, tossed, wedged, stuffed, and buried from one end to the other. These were whisked off to the washing machine immediately. In our rummaging around, we found some drug paraphernalia, including some pipes, papers, and a couple of bongs. This was a reminder of one of the less pleasant aspects of our relationship with Peter. For several years we had periodically done battle over his use of dope. It was a problem that had caused all three of us considerable pain and at times threatened to drive us completely apart. Whatever dope accessories, as well as other junk, we found, went directly into the garbage pail. In fact, we had enough to fill both pails. Luckily, the garbage man would be coming that morning. I thought, *"At least the timing is good,"* and was surprised at the feeling of self-loathing that flooded through me. I guess the tough-minded, cynical approach wasn't working.

As we were working in his room, I became aware of a problem that was to remain with me for months, and to an extent is still with me today. I found it extremely difficult to go into Peter's room. I felt like an intruder; I was violating his privacy. I was there without permission. We had respected his privacy for the most part when he was alive. When he was home, we never entered without knocking; when he was out, we didn't enter. The only exceptions were when Suzanne made a dirty-clothes foray, or I hunted for something of mine, often a tool, which he had borrowed and not returned. Now, to be searching through his possessions seemed to be abrogating the unspoken contract we had with him.

"I'd better make some coffee," I said. "Sally and Gardiner will be here any minute." I had been wondering where they were because it had been some time since I had called. I went downstairs to make the coffee, glad to be out of Peter's room but feeling guilty at being glad.

In a while Suzanne came down with another load of wash. "Are they here yet?" she asked. As it was now about six-thirty, we debated calling them again. They were usually late for engagements, but under the circumstances I couldn't understand their delay. We decided to give them a little longer before we phoned a second time.

Suzanne said that she had a pain in her stomach. Not exactly pain, but she felt sick to her stomach. Also, she was trembling slightly. I asked her if she was all right. She said she was, although her mouth was terribly dry. She still had not cried; neither had I, for that matter. I got her a couple of sodium bicarbonate tablets and took some myself. My stomach wasn't doing too well either.

The reason we had these tablets was itself a source of sadness. Peter had for years wanted a dog. I had grown up with dogs and knew that having a dog was like having a two-year-old child. Dogs, for example, require attention to a much greater degree than cats. We had had a succession of cats since Peter was three. Although they were family pets, Peter had named them. First was David (after his uncle who brought the cat to us), next was Leo (after Leo the Lion), and then Martha (after Martha Mitchell, of all things). David died under anesthesia while being neutered, Leo died of cystitis, and Martha was run over. By the time we moved to Connecticut we had three others: Boris, Robert, and Solo. Boris, one of the most engaging cats I have ever known died from a virus in the summer of 1978.

In 1977, our house had been broken into and virtually every portable item of value stolen. Our neighbors were not robbed. It was pointed out to me that our neighbors had a big dog. The implied logic, specious or not, added to the old argument that every boy should have a dog, finally wore me down. I tried to save face by mumbling something about the two of them assuming full responsibility for the mutt. Instead of a mutt, however, we wound up with a bull terrier.

Originally bred in the early nineteenth century in England for bull-baiting, the bull terrier easily adapted to dogfighting when Parliament outlawed the baiting of bulls, bears, and other animals. For all that, these medium-size dynamos make marvelous pets if treated and trained properly. Peter early on decided that he wanted one. Thus, we wound up with Maplewood Lady Phoebe.

I quickly realized that Phoebe and Peter were well mated, a case of "elective affinities," I suppose. Among other qualities they shared were medium size, well-developed muscularity, playfulness, toughness, and a willful disobedience. Sadly, in March 1979, we found out that Phoebe was dying from a chronic kidney disease. Upon our vet's advice, we took her to Yale–New Haven Hospital (they have a veterinary clinic for serious illnesses) for further tests. The prognosis was the same: she had at most perhaps a year to live. We were given various medicines to use as her condition deteriorated. Among them were sodium bicarbonate pills. By July she had failed to the point where living was an obvious burden to her. I took her to our vet, and he confirmed my belief that she should put down. I am convinced that she knew she was dying. As I lifted her onto the examining table, she wagged her tail weakly and, with resigned understanding in her eyes, gave me a goodbye look. I held her and patted her head while the vet administered sodium pentobarbital. Within seconds she was dead, just ten days before Peter was to die. So even something as trivial as taking a pill had poignant implications for us.

I had the sense that we were treading water. Without consciously thinking about it very clearly, I knew that we had a great deal to do that morning and for the next few days as well. There were arrangements to be made, people to phone, people to see. There was also a need, unrealized at the time, to have people—friends and relatives—around us. I didn't know if we could make it, but instinctively I sensed that we certainly couldn't make it alone. In the face of something this monstrous we needed help and support—all we could get.

It was still too early to do anything beyond that which had already been done. The official machinery had been put into gear, and the rest would have to wait for business hours. There was no point in waking other friends or family, some of whom lived as far away as California. All we could do for now was wait. Just wait.

At last Sally and Gardiner arrived. They looked dreadful. Faces drawn and bloodless, they seemed to move slowly as if burdened by a great weight. Sally's eyes were red and swollen. We met by the garage. I don't remember anyone speaking; we just held each other, all four of us in one embrace. There were tears, of course, but no words; they would have been superfluous.

For the first time Suzanne cried a little. But her tears were stilled by a feeling of absolute emotional pain that was actually physical. This was quickly followed by a sense of panic. She experienced a combination of terror and disbelief that led to a disorienting sense of unreality. She felt as though there had been an explosion inside her, that her heart had somehow been damaged. Outwardly, however, she appeared perfectly calm, quite normal in fact.

Already the day was unpleasantly hot and extremely muggy; the atmosphere seemed to cling to you. We had coffee outside in the early light while we talked about what had happened and made plans about what needed to be done. Sally had brought some tranquilizers and sleeping pills. Suzanne and I took a couple of Valiums, and I bummed a cigarette from Gardiner. I had stopped smoking two years before, but for the past few hours I had been craving a cigarette. If one can use a word like *enjoy* under the circumstances. I thoroughly enjoyed that cigarette, and the others I bummed as well.

We had decided that Peter would be cremated and his ashes interred in our family plot in Colorado Springs (points Big Peter was to agree with), and that we would have a memorial service on Friday. Gardiner suggested that since summer school was in session, it would be helpful if the service were held in the afternoon. That was fine with us, so we settled on four o'clock as a convenient time for people who were working. He and Suzanne started working on an obituary. Suzanne said she didn't want flowers, so they decided to establish a scholarship fund at King in Peter's name. It seemed a bit ironic to me, since Peter liked school about as much as he liked cleaning his room or eating liver, but he had been relatively happy at King and had had a fair amount of athletic success, as well as a number of good friends. When they had finished, Gardiner read the obituary to me. It sounded fine, insofar as an obituary can sound anything but terrible.

I heard a car and saw that it was our neighbors'. Although their house is well set back from ours, we share a common driveway. Doris was taking Michael to the station to catch the commuter train to New York. I broke the news to them. In a way it seemed to be getting easier to tell people; I had no difficulty getting the words out. In fact, I had a sense of removal from the situation. It was as though I were standing aside, detached and removed, watching myself talking to them. I was to experience this *displacement* quite often in the days to come.

Doris said she would come right back after dropping Michael at the station. She told us later that Michael was terribly upset and wanted to stay, but she had convinced him he would be better off going to work. He could catch an earlier train home if he wished.

We then made lists of people to contact. Working together, we decided whom each of us would call. It was amazing how well we were able to function, how clearheaded we were. For example, Suzanne remembered that she was supposed to drop off her car at the garage before work and be picked up there by a co-worker. She called Jan at home to cancel and gave her our sad news. In fact, immersing ourselves in the practical and even trivial details was a godsend. It was of immense help in getting through the first few terrible days.

We made a few more calls. I phoned my sister in New York and my cousin in Colorado, so she could be with my eighty-three-year-old aunt, Eleanor, whom I would call later. Suzanne called her brothers, Tom and David. We found these calls extremely difficult because we were breaking into their everyday routines and bringing pain.

It was now a little after eight. Suzanne called Dale. Dale is a psychoanalyst whom we had been seeing for some years. We'd started going to him while undergoing a crisis in our marriage. We'd continued to see him individually because we found psychoanalysis a helpful method for finding out about ourselves. After our relationship with Peter reached a crisis, he also started seeing Dale.

Dale is quite an extraordinary man. A Presbyterian minister, he had undergone psychoanalysis years ago and decided that he could be of more help through that discipline than through religion. Although essentially a Freudian, he is actually quite eclectic in his approach to therapy. We have found him immensely helpful, so it was quite natural that he should be one of the first people we turned to. Dale was utterly shocked when Suzanne told him. I had gotten on the other phone, but I remember very little of the conversation. I had a Wednesday afternoon session, and Dale said he felt it was vitally important that I keep the appointment and that Suzanne should share the session. We were not too enthusiastic about the idea. Dale said to think it over, and he would call back later in the day.

Doris returned and brought over a pot of coffee she had

made. Joyce, who worked with Suzanne at the Stamford Health Department arrived, and, after sitting with us a while, did some more laundry. Doris pointed out that we would probably have a lot of people stopping by, so we would need to have some food on hand. She and Joyce took charge of that area. It was a good thing they did, because people came—colleagues of mine from school, colleagues of Suzanne's from the health department, friends of Peter's, family friends, acquaintances, and even a stranger or two who had suffered a similar loss and wanted to comfort us.

Meanwhile, Suzanne had been making more calls. She phoned Coral, whose birthday it had been that night, and Greg, who had gone swimming with Peter at the reservoir. She also called Babs, with whom we had shared a house some years ago after her husband Frank committed suicide. Babs was tied up because she was getting one of her sons ready for a trip to France to visit relatives. Her oldest boy, Frank, who was one of Peter's best friends, would be up for the service. As soon as she had gotten Michael off, however, she would come. She would also notify some of our friends on Long Island, where we had lived for eight years. Additionally, she was going to try to locate an old and dear friend who had lost her only son ten years ago. Aunt Sally Bowers, as Peter had called her virtually from the time he could talk, is a remarkable woman whose sensitivity, understanding, and compassion were to be of enormous help to us.

For the rest of the morning we made more phone calls, in between talking with people who had stopped by. Greg and Coral arrived. We sat outside with them, seeking what shade we could to avoid the blistering sun. *"I could use less sun and more son,"* I thought. *"Why am I playing word games at a time like this?"* Greg was nearly catatonic. Coral kept repeating, "I've lost my best friend." It was evident that we weren't the only ones who needed help. It struck me forcefully how terrible this must be for the kids. They were just beginning to find out what life was about, beginning to discover some of the difficulties of living, and now they were faced with the problem of death. A grandmother or an uncle had lived their lives, so to speak, but a seventeen-year-old. . . . How does one explain the incomprehensible? They were beginning to realize that Time held them green and dying, as Dylan Thomas once noted.

Big Peter phoned. He was with his family, and some other relatives would be there soon. He had made arrangements with a funeral home in Stamford because he knew one of the chaps there. Peter would be picked up any time now. We discussed plans for the funeral home. We agreed we didn't want a wake, but we did want members of our families to be able to see Peter if they wished. We also wanted it restricted to members of the family. Suzanne insisted that the coffin be closed. We finally settled for having it closed, but it could be opened for those who wanted to see him.

By now it was late morning. Greg's and Coral's mothers came by. They were both nicely dressed. Suzanne was wearing an old, faded, well-worn sundress. She was aware of the incongruity but was not bothered by it. She sensed that there were many things once considered important that would no longer bother her.

Before he returned to school, Gardiner phoned the newspapers to give them the obituary. He needed gas but gas was being rationed: this was an odd day and his license plate ended in an even number. I decided to drop Suzanne's car off for its needed repair, so Gardiner followed me to my service station. Luckily, there was only a short line. While Gardiner got in line, I explained our problem. They were horrified and of course there would be no difficulty; Gardiner would get his gas, and Suzanne's car would be ready by three o'clock. I was aware of a feeling of discomfort, as though I were using Peter's death to gain preferential treatment. I walked over to Gardiner, who was now at the pumps. The gas line had grown quite sizable. A couple of people had noticed his plate and were watching us rather hostilely—or so it seemed to me. I was ready to belt the first person who challenged us. I was almost hoping someone would.

Gardiner explained to me why he and Sally had taken so long. After he had gotten off the phone, he had staggered into the bathroom feeling deathly ill. He had felt as though he were burning up. He had sat on the edge of the bathtub for some time before he felt even remotely normal again. He had then told Sally. She had been devastated. Naturally, they had needed some time to deal with the shock and pull themselves together before they came to us. I felt like a heel for not having anticipated this.

When I got back home, two more friends of Suzanne's from the health department, Reed and Rita, had arrived. I noticed that Suzanne was crying. This was one of the benefits of seeing friends. Whenever someone new expressed sympathy, Suzanne would cry. Seeing someone else suffering and offering comfort shook her out of her shock, her emotional lethargy, and she got in touch with her feelings. Also, having to give details of what had happened helped to crack the shell that shock had been building around her emotions. Pain was brought out into the open.

Joyce, who had been listening, said, "How can you keep telling the story over and over? Just hearing the raw facts hurts *me* so much. What is it doing to *you?*" Certainly, it was painful to recount the details, but the pain was there anyway. But we knew what she meant. In some ways it's almost easier to hurt for yourself than for others.

Joyce had good reason to be upset. In one of life's nasty ironies, she and Suzanne had been bitching about their sons the previous day. They had spoken of how angry they were with them, how the boys were always doing something stupid or thoughtless, how they were constantly screwing up in one way or another, causing needless apprehension for their parents. Suzanne had said that if Peter lived to grow up he would probably be a fine person, because he'd worked out so much in his teenage years. They'd also talked about the newly acquired moped and what a battle it would be to get Peter to wear a crash helmet. Joyce's oldest son, who was Peter's age, had a moped, on which he'd recently had an accident and broken his arm. Thus, Peter's death and his manner of dying had special impact for Joyce.

Dale called back and reemphasized the importance of our coming in to see him. I said that I was reluctant and had no relish for the drive into the city. I'd probably put us into a ditch. He said simply, "You can do it." The question of Suzanne's viewing Peter also came up. Dale said he thought she should, but we could talk about it when we saw him.

25

It was so uncomfortably hot by this point that we moved indoors. We sat in the living room with the curtains drawn and a fan going. Someone said that we should get some rest before we went into New York. After all, we had been up since the middle of the night, practically. I pointed out that it was like an oven upstairs. Doris suggested that we borrow a spare air conditioner of hers for the bedroom. Sleeping would be difficult enough for us without having to cope with the miserable, humid heat we were experiencing. Reed and I lugged it over from her house and installed it in one of the bedroom windows.

As we finished, I wondered why we had never bought one ourselves. It was one of those articles we could afford, but for some reason we never felt we could. Actually, I thought I knew the reason. If we'd had one, then Peter would have wanted one also. Certainly, we couldn't have afforded two. How could we justify having one for our comfort while he didn't? Just another source of friction, I figured. Also, we had a fan, and by unspoken agreement he had used it at night during hot spells from the time he was a small child. Maybe I couldn't feel so noble and self-sacrificing if we'd had an air conditioner while he'd had only a fan.

I called the Episcopal church to find out if it would be available Friday afternoon. It was, but the rector was out of town. I was given the name of a priest who was covering in his absence. I told Suzanne, and it was then that she suggested that Dale should co-officiate at the service. We would ask him when we saw him that afternoon.

The air conditioner had cooled our bedroom by this point, so Doris and Joyce persuaded Suzanne to lie down for a while. She rested for about an hour, but couldn't sleep. Earlier, Joyce had finished with the laundry. She had taken Peter's clothes out to her car, thinking she would spare Suzanne the pain of seeing them. Suzanne had seen her and said that it wasn't necessary. Now his clothes were neatly placed on a bed in the guest room. She asked me to pick out the ones we wanted him to be wearing. She had to go to Stamford, so she would take them to the funeral home. Suzanne and I had decided to use the type of clothing Peter had chosen to wear in life. He had a great many rock-group T-shirts. His favorite group had been the Grateful Dead. I instinctively picked one up. Joyce looked slightly taken aback. I said, "This should be appropriate, don't you think?" She looked very taken aback. I settled on a less provocative one and a pair of jeans.

I phoned the funeral director. I was concerned that they might not be able to make Peter presentable for viewing. I knew that modern undertaking techniques could, in a manner of speaking, work miracles, but Peter had been quite severely damaged. Even through the darkness and my own shock I had been able to see that the back of his skull had been crushed and that his face had suffered some damage. There had been a great deal of blood, but that, I realized, can be misleading to a layman. I was assured that they could "restore" him quite nicely. Further, I could inspect him myself and decide then if he was fit to be seen. I agreed and requested that they keep the makeup to the barest minimum. I'd once seen a close friend who had been made to look like an eighteenth-century fop. The undertaker assured me they would, but, once again, I could judge for myself.

Doris and Joyce had bought all sorts of cold cuts,

cheeses, salads, and breads. As it was now after midday, Doris said we should eat some lunch. She fixed Suzanne a plate, but I managed to find something to do in order to avoid eating. The thought of food made my stomach turn over. I had been drinking coffee and smoking cigarettes all morning; they seemed to be all I needed.

I was on my way to the kitchen for another cup of coffee when Doris waved a plate of food at me, but I was spared further dissemblance by the arrival of Sally Bowers. It turned out she had been visiting friends in Westchester, where she had been tracked down by her mother, who had been contacted by Babs. She'd hopped in her pickup truck and come right over. I had known Sally since we were fifteen, and, though we would not see each other for years at a time, we remained close friends. Through a mutual friend, Dave, she had met Suzanne long before I knew there was a Suzanne. In fact, it was through Sally and Dave's "good offices" that I met Suzanne in the first place.

Sally had Suzanne and Peter as weekend guests when I first met them. He was two and a half, and I took to him immediately. I was sitting in the living room when he appeared in the doorway, fresh from his bath. He was wearing his Dr. Denton's, which bulged ridiculously in the middle because of his diapers. When Suzanne told him to say hello to me, he marched over, thrust out his paw, and in a surprisingly deep and husky voice said, "How do you do?" The look in his eyes, however, suggested that neither of us should take this courtliness too seriously.

I was so impressed with his manners that I began referring to him as the Little Gent—a practice I was soon forced to abandon when he tried to bite me. Suzanne attempted to pass it off as a gesture of affection, but Sally, having recently been on the receiving end of one of these "gestures," took a slightly different view. Nonetheless, I decided then and there that this guy was all right. In the months to come, he was to make Suzanne more attractive in my eyes; he played no small part in my convincing myself that I wanted to marry her.

Sally's son, Jeb, as I noted earlier, had died ten years before. He had been killed in a freakish car accident. He had been riding in the back of a convertible. The top had been down, and, when the car had skidded on an ice patch, Jeb had been thrown into a telephone pole and killed instantly. Although he had been a couple of years older than Peter, they had been fairly good friends and for brief periods had seen a lot of each other. Peter was seven at the time of Jeb's death, and, although he couldn't articulate his feelings very well, he had been deeply moved by it. I know it took Suzanne and me a long time before Jeb's death and Sally's suffering receded from our everyday awareness. So Sally and we were bound not only by our friendship and shared experience but also by shared tragedy.

We had not seen Sally for several years, but when she walked in the door it was as if we had just seen her the day before. She's that kind of person. We talked a long time. What we said was not so important; I don't even remember most of the conversation. What was important was that Sally was there.

CHAPTER

2

DALE LIVES on the Upper West Side, so it only takes a little over an hour to drive there from Wilton. Driving in proved to be no problem at all, nor did the performance of any other routine functions. Except for a pervasive sense of grief, I felt perfectly normal. My mind was clear and sharp, and the only difference I noticed was a heightened awareness and a growing sense of unspecified self-consciousness.

It was good to see Dale. I felt warmed by his welcome. I thought how different this was from my customary reaction to seeing him. Generally, I dread my individual sessions. I find the struggle to get in touch with feelings and childhood experiences that I've spent a lifetime repressing incredibly painful. Dale, of course, assumes the role of the tormentor who forces me to put myself on the analytical rack each week. So I usually feel that I'm playing the accused heretic to Dale's Torquemada as he ushers me into his office. But this time he was simply a friend and fellow sufferer.

We went over details again, filling Dale in on points that had not been mentioned in our phone conversation. He told us that when we had called the first time, he had had a patient with him who knew Suzanne and Peter and me quite well. He said the two of them just cried and sought solace in each other's company. We explained that we were going to have a memorial service on Friday afternoon, and we would very much like Dale to co-officiate. We discussed this for a while before he agreed to do it. For one thing, it is an unshakable tenet of Dale's that one never acts without first discussing the reasons or motives for the intended action. Also, he was concerned that we might have difficulty dealing with a switch in roles on his part from analyst to clergyman. As much as he would like to do it, he would not if it might interfere with our analysis. Suzanne pointed out that in such an extraordinary circumstance as this, that should not be a problem. Anyway, she continued, this would not be a social occasion but more of a ceremonial one. The point here is that Dale has always been scrupulous about maintaining a professional distance between himself and his patients. Aside from Christmas parties at the end of group sessions, he never socialized with us. Although we consider him a friend, ours is a friendship with clearly defined boundaries.

Dale asked about the arrangements we had made at the funeral home. We said that Peter would be readied Thursday for those who wanted to see him. On Friday he would be cremated. Dale wanted to know what time they would be removing him, because he couldn't get up until Friday, and he needed to see Peter. He stressed that I should make the point to the funeral director that we wanted Friday morning as well as Thursday. I said I'd find out and phone him.

Dale then explained why it was important for him to see Peter, and why he felt it was crucial for Suzanne to see him. During World War II his brother had been killed. Naturally, under the circumstances, he had not been able to see his brother's body. To this day he has had difficulty accepting the fact of his brother's death. On an emotional level, at least, his brother's death has been left unresolved. For one thing, he explained, a part of us refuses to believe that a loved one is dead. Consequently, we need the graphic physical evidence of seeing the dead body to help us come to terms with this *unacceptable* fact. It is a necessary step in the grieving process.

I had seen Peter on the roadside, so Dale wasn't as concerned about me as he was about Suzanne. Nonetheless, he thought it would be wise for me to see him again, to go through the ceremonial procedure. To his mind, however, it was absolutely essential for Suzanne to see Peter. Suzanne was crying by this point. "But Dale," she said, "I can't. I just can't."

"Why not?" Dale asked.

"I couldn't bear it," she replied. "The idea terrifies me."

I noticed that her hands were clenched into fists so tightly that her knuckles were white. I felt emotionally dead myself, probably too frightened at feeling her terror.

"You know," Dale told her, "there's a good reason why cultures have developed elaborate mourning rituals over the years. It's not just ignorance or religious superstition.

The point is to help us with the grieving process. If we don't grieve, if we don't fully face the fact of a loved one's death, we don't really come to terms with that person's death. We can be abnormally and unhealthily affected by a death, often without being consciously aware of it. I think that seeing Peter is essential for your emotional, as opposed to your intellectual, acceptance that he is dead."

Although she was still clearly disturbed by the idea, Suzanne said she understood what Dale was saying. She would see Peter tomorrow.

As we were about to leave, Dale said he would be seeing me at my group session, wouldn't he? I said he would if Suzanne could come, but I wasn't leaving her alone for an hour and a half while I was being consoled by the group. For an *outsider* to attend a group session is a rare, if not unheard of, event. But then this was a rather special situation. Also, several of the people in my group knew both Suzanne and Peter, as we had attended a weekend family marathon session at Dale's home on Long Island. Others had at least met them briefly, in Dale's waiting room, from time to time. Dale said he would have to ask the group about it, but he himself had no objections.

There is an hour between my individual and group sessions. I usually killed the time by going to a coffee shop and reading. This day we got a cold drink and then walked along Riverside Drive. It was a beautiful late afternoon, with long shadows thrown by the tall trees that line the Drive. There is a thin strip of park between the Drive and the West Side Highway, and beyond is the Hudson River. In the park were joggers, lovers, and children, a couple of the kids playing with dogs. Oddly, it was very quiet—light traffic on the highway and a gentle, cooling breeze blowing from the river. Very lovely and peaceful. Yet we felt completely alienated. We felt separated from all that was going on around us. We might as well have been inhabitants of a different world, there was so little connection between us and them. Somehow, we were now different. This was the first time I was to experience what I call the Bereaved Parent Syndrome. It means, quite simply, that there are two classes of people: those who have lost a child and those who have not. We belong to an exclusive club and, unfortunately, there is only one criterion for membership.

We arrived back at Dale's deliberately late, so that the group would have had some time to talk after Dale broke the news to them. Also, I didn't want to see any of them in the waiting room until everyone had arrived and been informed. Dale asked Suzanne if she would wait a few minutes before she went in. They needed a little more time to absorb the shocking news.

There were seven people in my group. The newest of us had been there for about two years, so we all knew each other quite well. We met once a week for an hour and a half. We sat in a circle, and there were a few unbreakable rules. Everything had to be verbalized; there could be no acting-out. Smoking was not allowed either. There was an openness, an honesty, a self-exposure that one doesn't encounter outside of this kind of situation. We could be pretty tough and harsh on each other, but we could also be loving and understanding and supportive. We were all very much individuals, but we all had a strong sense of community, of the group.

As I said, Dale had told them about Peter, but he had

not yet mentioned Suzanne's joining our session. The air of shock and pain was palpable. A couple of them were crying and red-eyed. All of them seemed to be moving or, more exactly, talking in slow time. Or maybe it was just me. I don't remember a single word anyone said to me. I was again benumbed. I didn't know how to accept the sympathy I felt flowing over me. I didn't want it. I didn't want to be in this position in which I had to be the recipient of such sympathy. I guess I was denying.

Dale asked them about Suzanne's joining us. Someone said, "You mean she's outside now? My God, of course." It was immediately clear that everyone concurred, so I got Suzanne. As we came in, I noticed someone had placed another chair in the circle. My sense of removal was so great at this point that I felt like an usher in an unfamiliar theater escorting a stranger to her seat.

I have only a general sense of that session, no particulars, except that everyone was going to attend the service. That point was made emphatically clear. There was some discussion of details: time of the service, directions to the church, who would drive, and so on. What I do remember is the sympathy and the effort to give comfort. And the pain they each felt—pain for us and pain for them. I remember also the concern that some of them expressed for Suzanne, for her state of mind, for her welfare. This was not at my expense, you understand, for in a situation like this I think one tends to look to the mother. Moreover, Suzanne's presence in our group tended to make her the center of attention. When the session was over, we all embraced, and Suzanne and I left for home. But first we wanted to stop at the Mitchells'—Peter's paternal grandparents—in Old Greenwich.

Big Peter was there, as were his sister and her family from Atlanta, as well as several other relatives. Again we were surrounded by warmth and concern and, of course, grief. But I felt strangely disconcerted. It took me a while to discover the reason. I had known the Mitchells for years, and all of them had from the beginning made me feel welcome, indeed, had treated me as one of the family. I remember once, years ago, Mrs. Mitchell had introduced me to someone not simply as Suzanne's husband but as "Peter's other father." It was a lovely gesture and indicated their acceptance of me. Big Peter and I had always gotten along well because, although I knew them slightly through Dave and Sally Bowers, he and Suzanne had separated and were a dead issue well before I came into her life. So why, I wondered, was I now feeling so troubled?

From the kitchen came the sound of laughter and ice cubes clinking in a glass, and I knew the source of my problem. In the past my only experience with a gathering of the Mitchell clan had been on festive holiday occasions such as Christmas. I associated their house with laughter and merrymaking. But now that single burst of laughter echoed through my mind like the report of a discharged weapon, for there was no merrymaking and very little laughter in this house now. That laugh penetrated the defenses my mind had been building around itself against the onslaught of grief that was attacking it. The atmosphere in this house was now so different from the one to which I was accustomed that I was momentarily left defenseless, completely exposed. The emotional camouflage I had hidden behind in the group had been stripped away. It was one of those moments when the full enormity of the event completely captured my consciousness, my sensibility. I had an absolute understanding, as though there were a synthesis of heart and mind, intellect and emotion, of the dreadful, irrevocable finality of Peter's death. It passed fairly quickly, for I don't think the mind could have survived if it hadn't. But it left me weak and dazed.

I tried to get out of myself by turning to others. Dr. Mitchell, Peter's grandfather, was sitting by himself, stone-faced and silent. He was removed from the rest of us. I wondered if with Peter's death he might not be reliving an earlier tragedy. His eldest son, Abner, had been killed in a motorcycle accident when in his early twenties. Mrs. Mitchell had an almost pathological dread of motorcycles. I remember she once said to us, when Peter was still a small child, that, whatever else we did, we shouldn't ever let him have a motorcycle. How ironic. We had let him get the moped as a compromise because he had desperately wanted a motorcycle. Both his uncles had had cycles years ago, and Peter had loved nothing more than to be whizzed around the backroads of Greenwich by either Tom or David.

As he grew older, he'd remained wild about motorcycles. One of his favorite posters had been of a group of motorcross cyclists tearing through the desert. He had been after us since he had gotten his license to let him have a cycle. He even had a crash helmet. But, partly out of consideration for Mrs. Mitchell and partly out of our own fear, we had steadfastly refused. And then they came out with those goddamned mopeds.

But I knew I couldn't really blame the moped. Peter and motor vehicles had never been a great combination. In the past year he'd had two accidents, although neither had actually been his fault. When he was fifteen, however, an incident occurred involving Suzanne's car, which became a kind of microcosm of our relationship.

Suzanne and I had gone to a dinner party at a friend's house. Just as dinner was ending, we got a phone call from Peter. I took the phone and Peter said. "Dad, I blew it." He was phoning from the police station. He'd taken Suzanne's VW Beetle, and gotten caught by the police. They were holding him until we came to claim him.

When we got there, the police explained that Peter had run a stop sign. He'd been seen by a patrol car, which had started after him. Peter had tried to outrun the cop. He'd failed to negotiate a sharp curve and hit the curb, blowing a tire. Luckily, that had been all the damage. As Peter had had Phoebe, the dog, with him, the cop had driven him to our house, where he'd allowed Peter to leave her before taking him to the police station.

The cop said Peter had been going close to seventy-five at one point. We were appalled at the idea of his driving the rickety old bug at that kind of speed on poorly maintained country roads. As the cop had already gotten the license plate number, he'd backed off because he was worried that Peter would lose control of the car. Back at the station they'd tried to put the fear of God into him, the cop said, by placing him in a holding cell. As the officer finished speaking, private enemy number one was brought in, not looking very formidable, and released to our tender mercies.

Two points were abundantly clear even at the time. We didn't know what was going on in his life. He had been taking Suzanne's car for some time, because he plainly knew how to drive. He would only admit to driving up and down the driveway, but we didn't believe him. And, once again, he'd pushed beyond the limits: he couldn't wait for the proper time.

A few weeks later we had to go to court, where a judge gave him a long, stern lecture of the type I was so good at. He placed Peter on probation, and we subsequently had the uplifting experience of being visited by a probation officer, who came to check on the reformation of Little Caesar. I think I was more enraged at Peter for causing an outsider to stick his nose into our family affairs than I was alarmed at his irresponsible behavior. As it was, we didn't allow Peter to get his driving license for several months past his sixteenth birthday. I doubted that this would accomplish much, but it's hard to break the habit of punishing unsatisfactory conduct.

I talked with Dr. Mitchell a while or, more exactly, I talked *to* him. It was a strange conversation. He remained torpid, responding but not initiating. He was immobilized by his grief and no one, including me, could comfort him. Mrs. Mitchell told me that they were very concerned about him. She took me aside to ask me how Suzanne was doing. I said quite well really, much as she was right now—deeply injured but functioning. We agreed to meet at the funeral home the next day.

There were several people at our house when we returned, in addition to Doris and Sally Bowers. Doris had made a list of people who had phoned. There were quite a few. One of them was my sister. I called her. She had forgotten the gist of our morning conversation; namely, that she would phone our aunt on Staten Island as well as her daughter in New Hampshire and her son in Massachusetts. She would tell them the service was to be on Friday, and I would either call her back with the time, or they could phone me. It shows the strange way shock affects people. She had thought she was being very level-headed and practical but, in fact, remembered little beyond the fact that Peter was dead.

This time we also discussed our mother. She was at this time in a hospital on Long Island with a fractured hip. We agreed that I should tell her personally, but there was no way I could get down there for a couple of days, probably not until Monday. I disliked keeping the news from Mother, but as she was literally bedridden, I saw no help for it. I felt that I had to be with her when she found out. Through circumstances, she was completely isolated, so I wasn't worried about her learning from someone else.

Suzanne was talking with our visitors in the living room while I was on the phone. Doris asked me if she could get me something to eat. I said we'd grabbed a bite in town. I've always thought I was a pretty good liar, but somehow she didn't seem convinced that I'd eaten. She was too considerate to make an issue of it, but she pointed out that whether or not I felt hungry, I simply had to get some food into me. I tossed a sandwich of some sort together.

By the time everyone had gone, we were emotionally exhausted. Sally Bowers went to bed, and Suzanne said we should too. I didn't want to. Although I was tired, I was afraid I wouldn't be able to sleep. The thought of lying in bed with no distractions to keep me from feeling fully the loss of Peter was more alarming than I cared to admit. But Suzanne said she was frightened to go upstairs alone, so I went with her.

Immediately after Peter's death—and for months to come—she became terrified of going upstairs alone or even being alone in the house. She was seized with an irrational terror that his ghost would appear.

Suzanne was fairly sure that she understood the reason for this fear. Her father had died when she was seven. As her mother had been eight months pregnant at the time, her doctor had told her not to attend either the wake or the funeral. It had also been found "inappropriate" for Suzanne to attend. Her father had been buried in his tuxedo, and she'd heard that this important figure in her life had looked wonderful.

Later, she'd gone to the cemetery with her mother to see her father's grave. In an effort to console her, Suzanne's mother had said, "Think that he's away on a trip." Since her father had often traveled on business, but had always returned, her child's mind had surmised that he would return this time as well. But return in what form? Decomposed, in a tuxedo? As a skeleton? For years she'd had nightmares about that.

Now, to her horror, the question arose, would the decomposed remains of her son be waiting, empty-eyed, at the top of the stairs? Emotionally, Suzanne had awaited her father's return for years because she'd never resolved his death, and now she was paying the price.

I think we may have taken sleeping pills that first night, but I'm not sure. In any case, we slept, but the nightmares came before the sleep. Suzanne was bombarded with ghastly images, ugly flashes, distortions. A huge head with great hunks of flesh missing, blood everywhere—blood flowing and blood congealed. Flashing red lights in the dark, pitch darkness, threatening darkness. A crowd around the telephone pole, police radios with their beeps and static and distorted voices. More blood, dark and rich, but useless, lifeless. Terror. Fear of sleep, fear of nightmares, fear of waking. Fear of waking up and starting all over again—another day, more pain, more horror. It really is true. Peter is dead, my son is dead, my baby is dead. It really is true. . . .

For some reason I kept thinking of Dale's insistence that Suzanne see Peter tomorrow to remove all emotional doubts. Probably the sensible thing to do. Dale is usually right. Helpful to Suzanne. Not necessary for me. I saw him already. Lucky thing I did when I did, one of the cops had said. I'd forgotten that. Peter didn't have his wallet with him. But he did have the driver's license of another boy who was eighteen. I hadn't known he'd had one but wasn't surprised. I'd had one myself as a kid in case I got carded in a bar. If I hadn't shown up they would have notified that other family. But I had identified him. Of course it was *him* I had identified. I couldn't have made a mistake. Absurd. Yet it was dark and he was a mess and I was upset. But it was so near our house, home. And the moped. Surely that was his moped. Coincidence? The world is full of extraordinary coincidences. Was it actually him? Beyond all reasonable doubt? I had to see him tomorrow. . . .

3

THURSDAY BEGAN as hot and humid as Wednesday had been. The air was so thick and heavy you nearly had to chew it in order to swallow. We had both slept somewhat fitfully, but luckily had always been able to get back to sleep fairly quickly, thanks in part to the air conditioner. Thursday also brought a renewal of Wednesday's feelings and a sense that here was another day to get through. It was helpful to know that it would be a busy one with plenty to do to keep myself occupied. I went down to the kitchen to make coffee while Suzanne showered.

I had gotten into the habit of using the downstairs bathroom, mainly because the water pressure in the shower was stronger than it was upstairs, and I like a hard shower—a fire hose would be just fine with me. Suzanne and Peter used the upstairs bathroom for the most part. As she was showering, Suzanne was aware of how clean the bathroom was. Usually she found Peter's hair in the shower, on the tiles, and on the floor of the tub. The tops of the shampoo and cream rinse often would be off, and a wet towel crammed into the towel rack, so she would nag him about mess and waste. Now the bathroom was perfect, just the way she'd always wanted it. Only now she didn't want it that way. We would both encounter this kind of paradox frequently in the days and weeks to come.

Sally Bowers and I were drinking coffee when Suzanne came down. Except for puffiness around the eyes, she looked quite good. She said her throat was sore from holding back tears. She had been looking at herself in the mirror and wondering at how normal she appeared. "Why doesn't it show more?" she asked.

I asked her if she'd like a tranquilizer. Before she could answer, Sally jumped in.

"I'd think twice about using those if I were you."

"What?" replied Suzanne, a bit startled.

"All you're doing is putting off the inevitable. The deep feelings are there. You're just postponing having to feel them. Tranquilizers may help some now, but they won't later. Why put it off?"

Neither of us had a ready reply. We just looked at each other a moment and then looked at Sally. I knew instinctively that she was right. Why in the world hadn't I realized that myself? I wondered. I knew perfectly well that tranquilizers usually do more harm than good. I suppose, unthinkingly, I had a model in my mind, partly based on experience, of how people in our situation should act. One of the things they did, particularly women, was take tranquilizers. I remember when Frank committed suicide, Babs called us at once. We rushed right over. She was in bad shape, so one of my first chores was to roust her doctor, who raced over to give her a sedative. He also wrote a prescription for some tranquilizers. That's the way it's done. But Sally's comment cut through all that nonsense and made me understand what I had failed to see myself. Maybe I hadn't wanted to see it, of course. Maybe I had been hoping to avoid some of the pain. As with so many unpleasant things, put them off and perhaps they won't have to be dealt with.

"You mean you didn't use any when Jeb died?" Suzanne asked.

"Not a thing," Sally said. "I can see the need if you're coming completely unglued, if you absolutely can't handle it." She paused a moment. "But you're handling it, aren't you?"

We were and, of course, she was right. Her quiet common sense carried the day. We took no more tranquilizers or sleeping pills.

Doris came over, and by nine or ten o'clock things were in full swing again, with the phone ringing and people stopping in.

Our friend Jane came over laden down with a meatloaf and a large pan of lasagna. We had called Jane and Michael the night before. That morning, Michael had had to go to New York. Jane had gone to the market and then home to cook. In the middle of sweating and almost passing out from the heat, she'd realized that what she was doing was absurd. She could have made something that was relatively cool to prepare. She figured it was the kind of crazy thing you do when you are more upset than you realize. Also, she'd realized that it was a way

45

to make herself suffer too. It might have been a way of combating the sense of helplessness felt by someone in the face of another's tragedy.

It cost Jane a lot to come over that morning. Not only is she an empathic person by nature, but also she had experienced several deaths, including her parents', within the past couple of years and had not fully worked out her own grief. She was also a little alarmed at how calm we had sounded on the phone.

Doris had made more coffee, so we drank that and talked. Afterward, Jane drove me to my gas station to get my car. On the way, she remarked that she had declared herself an enemy of death some time ago. She said she hated everything about it and thought the best way to deal with it was to get furious. I knew she was right and realized I hadn't begun to get in touch with the rage I felt both at Peter's death and at him for dying. I started to blame yesterday's tranquilizers but recognized that I was kidding myself. I have been terrified of my rage for so long that I don't need two tranquilizers to prevent myself from getting in touch with it.

When I returned home, I called the medical examiner. Unbelievably, I got him. He read me the cause of death. I asked him to translate it into understandable English. Peter had fractured his skull, crushed his brain, and snapped his spinal cord. The acute nature of his injuries would have caused death instantaneously. No, it was unlikely that wearing a crash helmet would have made a difference in this case, especially with the spinal column. I thanked him and rang off. I had learned what I wanted to know. Death had been virtually immediate. The police had told me that they suspected it must have been, but then I figured they usually said that. I know that in the army in Korea, commanding officers wrote that your son or husband died gallantly and with no suffering, even if the damn fool had been dead drunk, fallen down a latrine shaft, and slowly frozen to death buried in his comrades' waste.

I wanted to know, and I wanted Suzanne to be convinced of the truth of it, that Peter had not suffered. His death was bad enough without the appalling thought that his dying had been painful, even agonizing. At least we were spared that gruesome circumstance. The medical examiner had said that, even if Peter had been technically still alive for a couple of minutes, which he doubted, he would have been completely unconscious. I told Suzanne at once. Her tears this time were mostly those of gratitude and relief—as were mine.

More people came by. Among them were friends of ours, Mark and Linda, who have three children. They seemed quite subdued and stayed only about five minutes. I was beginning to feel like a doorman, ushering people in and out, dizzy from the constant flow. I did notice, however, that their exit was slightly abrupt. Some months later they explained why they'd left so quickly. They said that Peter's death had brought home to them their own vulnerability; they realized what it would be like if one of theirs died. It was so upsetting, they doubted they could be of any help to us. Also, they couldn't take all the people being there. "If it happened to us," Linda said, "we would be *alone*."

Several of Peter's friends arrived. Coral borrowed Peter's address book, saying she and Greg would use it to track down various other friends of Peter's. Someone told

Scott to show us the poem he had written about Peter. Suzanne read it and handed it to me. While she was talking with the kids, I read it, or rather, I tried to read it. The words danced on the page. They made no sense. I began again, angry that I couldn't comprehend what was, in fact, a fairly decent piece of writing. I still couldn't focus properly on it, but I did get the sense of an impressive honesty of feeling.

Suzanne took Clista upstairs so she could select a few of Peter's things. Clista and Peter had gone together for a while and remained friends after they had stopped dating. They had met when Clista had crashed her car into the back of Peter's as he was preparing to make a turn. A week or so later he'd taken her to see Charlie Daniels—her first rock concert. I'd teased her that she'd have to find a less violent way of meeting boys.

Suzanne and I had talked with Sally Bowers about the service and decided that we were going to pattern it partly on the one she had held for Jeb. That meant it was to be as positive and upbeat as such a service could be. I called the priest who was substituting for the vacationing rector. Bob Tate was in his late twenties and had been ordained within the past year or so. I outlined the service as we envisioned it, and he said he would choose some appropriate traditional passages to read. He was fully agreeable to having Dale share in officiating. We decided to meet at our house at twelve on Friday when we, including Dale, would work out the final details.

Suzanne needed a dress for Friday, so she and Sally Bowers were going to Darien to meet her sister at a dress shop. I had some things to do myself, such as going to the florist to arrange for the flowers we planned to use at the service. We decided to meet at the funeral home in Stamford at two. Suzanne impressed upon me that I shouldn't be late. I considered reminding her that *I* was the punctual one, but decided not to. I waved goodbye and broke into a sweat.

I watched the battered old pickup truck with Suzanne in the passenger seat pull into the parking lot. I was eager to see her. We had only been apart for two hours, but it seemed much longer. I felt a need to be with her, to have her physically present, such as I hadn't felt since the time I'd courted her, when every minute away from her had seemed like an hour. I knew that coming to the funeral home was an ordeal for her. It was obvious to others as well. Before I'd left the house, Doris had told me she was worried about Suzanne because she was so clearly terrified at seeing Peter. Suzanne seemed in fairly good shape, but I could sense the tension. Sally and her mother arrived and the five of us went in.

Most of the Mitchells were already there, as were Reed and another friend, Agnes, from New York. While Suzanne talked with them, I hunted for the director and introduced myself. He took me into the room where Peter was. It was a large room, probably fifty feet long. At the far end was an open casket with a body in it. We walked over, the body coming into clearer view the closer we got. It was Peter, all right. I had a feeling of complete unreality. I have seen a number of dead people and been to many wakes, but to see my own son laid out in a casket was too ridiculous to be real. I didn't feel panic nor was I distraught. I was simply disoriented. Part of my mind was saying this shouldn't be, this couldn't be. But it un-

49

mistakably was. Therefore, something was wrong, out of whack, screwy. My mind couldn't resolve the contradiction, the logical incongruity, with which I was faced. I felt as though a great cosmological joke had been played on me, but I was having trouble seeing the humor.

I was brought up short at the sight of Peter's scraggly beard. He had started it a few weeks before, and it wasn't an entirely successful effort. He had been quite proud of it, though, as I had been of my first one. I remembered now that the undertaker had asked me about it on the phone, and, knowing what it had meant to Peter, I had told him not to shave it. More important, Peter had liked it and I hadn't, so for me to have it removed would have been another, final attempt to impose my will upon him. Let people see him the way he wanted to be seen, not the way I wanted.

The undertaker broke in upon my thoughts. He said it was good that we decided to keep the beard as there was some swelling—or some cuts, I don't remember which —that they couldn't have concealed if Peter were shaved. He pointed out that they had kept the makeup to a minimum, as I had requested. He started indicating something else when I thought, *"Jesus Christ. He's proud of his work. He's like a salesman selling me something. No, more a craftsman attesting to the quality of his product. 'Now examine this chair, sir. Note the elegant line of the arm. . . .'"*

I became aware of a pronounced silence. He had finished speaking and was awaiting my reply. "Yes," I said. "That's fine. He looks fine. Thank you." We exchanged a few more words and he left. He was actually a very pleasant person to deal with. He was not at all unctuous, nor had he that artificial sympathy so common among those in his profession.

They had done a good job with Peter, and he was, as these things go, presentable. But I didn't like the way he looked. I could see now that his nose had been broken, and one of his lips was swollen. I wondered if he had lost any teeth. I had brought a gold signet ring of his father's that Peter often wore. His hands were clasped over his stomach. When I lifted his finger to put on the ring, I was surprised at its lack of rigidity and coldness. I put my hand on his forehead a moment; it was not as cold as I had expected it to be. I noticed that his chest was puffed up more than was natural. The result of the autopsy, I guessed. No, I didn't like the way he looked, not one goddamned little bit. He looked dead. I went out to get Suzanne. If she needed to see him dead, this should do the trick, I thought savagely.

Suzanne was busily talking to someone. I waited beside her for a while but, when she showed no sign of stopping, I gently took her elbow. She gave me a pleading look and turned back to continue talking.

"We're going in now," I said. "Okay?"

We walked over to the open doorway, I purposefully, Suzanne hesitatingly. As we were about to walk in, the director asked if we would like to be alone. I appreciated his consideration and was glad I hadn't been rude to him. He closed the door behind us. Holding Suzanne's arm, I took a step forward.

"Wait!"

She turned toward me and was clutching my arm so tightly I was beginning to lose sensation in it. I saw her looking out of the corner of her eye in the direction of the casket. She was holding me with both hands now.

"Don't rush me," she said.

"I won't," I said. "We'll take all the time you want."

We stayed like that for a few moments. Then I turned to her slowly until she was facing the far end of the room. She darted a quick glance in that direction.

"Oh, I can't!" she implored me.

"Yes, you can," I responded.

We took a few steps and then halted again.

"You can do it, Lovey," I told her. "It'll be okay."

We walked forward again. She was moving so stiffly and awkwardly it was as if she were just learning to walk. Her body was rigid with tension. Over five minutes had passed since we had entered, and we were still only halfway across the room.

"Don't let go of me," she pleaded.

"I won't. Don't worry. You're doing fine," I said. "Do you want to go back and sit down for a few minutes?"

"No. Let's keep going."

We were nearly there now; Suzanne was looking straight ahead. I was dreading the last few steps, but, after a short pause, she moved forward. As we got to the casket, I noticed that her eyes were averted. Then she looked directly into it. She gave a soft gasp and just stood looking. I felt her body relaxing.

"It's not Peter," she said.

"*Oh shit!*" I thought. "*What's this now?*"

She moved closer to him, then turned to me.

"That's just a body," she said. "That's not Peter. Now I know there's a spirit. That's just his body."

The shell in the coffin was ghastly to Suzanne. Peter had been beautiful but this thing was ugly. She felt that the only parts of his body that still resembled our son were the curly, brown hair; the muscular, brown wrestler's arms; and the tightly clasped hands. Those were Peter's hands all right, with some of the grease from the gas station still under his nails. The undertaker hadn't been able to remove it all.

When Suzanne moved to the head of the coffin, all she could see were his hands, arms, and hair. At that point, the shell became Peter. Maybe what made his face so different in life, she thought, was the glowing essence, or spirit, behind the mask. Maybe that's what people mean by soul.

"That's just his body," she repeated.

She was completely composed now. I sensed a feeling of peace come over her, the tension drained away. *"How right you were, Dale,"* I thought. She touched his hair, his face. She noticed the ring on his finger. I explained that I had brought it from home. She gave my hand a squeeze. We stayed a while longer, looking at him and occasionally talking. Just the three of us. Then I walked over to open the door so others could come in.

CHAPTER

4

WHEN WE GOT HOME, Suzanne said she wanted to walk up the road to the spot where Peter had been killed. "I've got to see it," she said.

"It's probably a bit messy," I told her. "Are you sure?"

She looked at me a moment. "Yes," she answered.

I understood her need and was no longer worried about exposing her to ugly realities. An ugly reality is easier to cope with than an ugly phantasm; the known is less threatening than the unknown. We were about fifty yards from the place when I pointed up the road.

"That's the pole," I said. "You can just make out the storm drain beyond it."

We continued walking. Just this side of the pole, I indicated where the moped had been. Some of the tall grass was trampled down. A couple of broken pieces of the moped were still there. I picked them up and threw them hard into the woods. It was very quiet and the sound of the pieces hitting the trees washed over us. We moved to the other side of the pole. Here the grass was completely crushed flat. In one indentation the matted grass was covered with congealed blood. In the late afternoon sun the blood seemed to shimmer as though it were alive and vital. Suzanne leaned down and for a moment I thought she was going to put her hand in it.

We moved to the storm drain and looked at the scar in the curbing just beyond it. The sequence of events kept recurring in my mind: the drain, the curb, the pole; the drain, the curb, the pole. Two seconds maximum, I reckoned. I looked at the pole. There was a slightly discolored spot, which might have been where he hit. I felt a surge of adrenaline. I wanted to strike the pole with a sharp ax. I wanted to feel the blade bite deeply into it. I wanted the sensation of feeling a powerful, well-aimed blow striking home. I wanted to hear that pole scream in agony as the ax bit into it. I wanted to destroy it, to obliterate it. Suzanne, almost as if sensing my mood, moved beside me, and, hand in hand, we headed home.

Doris was relieved to hear how well it had gone at the funeral home. There were more messages and more people came by. We were particularly touched when one of my colleagues, Ollie—King's Mr. Chips, who had retired the year before—and his wife, who was in poor health, came by. It was a combination of this kind of effort by others and people's need to comfort us that meant so much.

Although Ollie had never had Peter as a student—or perhaps, because he never had—he had clearly liked him. Probably it was Peter's athleticism that had drawn them together. Ollie had not only been a varsity athlete at Middlebury but also had been a truly superior coach at King. No longer coaching the past few years, he still attended most of our athletic events. A large man, chairman of the math department, and head of the upper school, he had been a formidable figure on campus. He had taught exclusively in the upper school, and Peter was probably one of the few middle schoolers he had known by name.

Ollie reminded me, as we talked that afternoon, of the time when Peter was in seventh or eighth grade, and he was leaving school early to fly to Atlanta. The year before, Big Peter had given him a baseball with Babe Ruth's autograph on it. Now, through Big Peter's business connections, they were going to get Hank Aaron's autograph on the same ball. While Peter was waiting by the front office to be driven to the airport, Ollie came out of his office and demanded to know what Peter was doing. Why wasn't he in class? When Peter explained, Ollie wanted to see the ball. Apparently, there was some teasing about Ollie's trustworthiness to actually hold the ball. When I came on the scene, the two of them were jabbering away and laughing at Ollie's anecdotes. I had to get back to class, but Ollie waited with him until his grandmother came for him. Ollie had impressed upon him that he should keep the ball in its plastic case and, above all, keep it out of sight, Peter told me later. He should resist any temptation to show off the ball, as someone might try to steal it. "You know," Peter had said to me, "Mr. Olsen is a really nice guy." Peter had always been a good judge of character.

After the Olsens left, Suzanne wanted to show me

the new dresses and get my opinion as to which she should wear. One was bright turquoise and the other lavender. She had deliberately avoided buying something somber. "I absolutely don't want anything funereal," she said. I agreed, but couldn't decide which dress looked worse on her. She finally gave up on me and went to Sally Bowers for her opinion. They chose the lavender one.

Early that evening Suzanne's brothers and their wives came over, as did Jane and Michael. There was a lot of food in the kitchen and several people snacked while Suzanne and Sally Bowers ate. I saw Doris coming my way, and, bowing to the inevitable, I headed for the kitchen.

The question of appetite is a curious one. I not only had no appetite those first few days, but I also found the thought and the taste of food repulsive. I don't know if it had to do with chemical changes in my system due to shock and grief, or if it had a psychological basis. Since eating is an instinctive life-preserving endeavor, I may have unconsciously resisted it. I may have been operating along the lines of "How can I try to remain alive when Peter is dead?" In any case, food repelled me, and I lost ten pounds in the first three or four days after his death.

Several of Peter's friends asked Suzanne if they could see Peter. She knew this was a need on their part, not idle curiosity. We'd restricted viewing to members of the family, but Suzanne felt it had been so helpful for her to see Peter that she told them to go ahead. She called the funeral home and informed them.

I looked out the front window and saw a young fellow coming up the driveway on his skateboard. I didn't know him, but there was something arresting, almost forlorn, about this solitary figure as he looked somewhat uncertainly toward the house. He came to the front door and introduced himself. He was a friend of Peter's, named Paul. He spent about half an hour with us. We admired his pluck in braving a group of unfamiliar adults. But his need to see us and express his feelings overcame any reservations he might have had.

Suzanne asked Jane and Michael if they would like to see Peter's room. This worried them because they wondered if we were going to turn his room into a shrine. They couldn't begin to imagine the pain involved in dismantling it, but there were therapeutic benefits in not keeping it as a monument. This was a question that bothered us as well. We, too, were aware of the danger of treating his room and possessions as hallowed. On the other hand, it would be heartless and unnecessary to simply remove all physical traces of him. Suzanne had already given a few of his things to some of his friends. Additionally, we had thrown out a great deal of junk. We had decided that whatever we did with his room could be done later; there was no imperative for immediate action.

While I was waiting for them to come down again, I realized I'd been doing a lot of waiting the past two days. Waiting for this person to arrive, for that one to leave, for us to go to one place or another. I was waiting to keep busy. Beyond that, I simply had a sense of waiting, but I had no idea for what. Later on, I understood: I was waiting for each step in the mourning ritual to take place; I was waiting for time to pass. I was waiting for an end to the pain, or at least a diminution of it.

After everyone had left, I was talking with Sally Bowers and Suzanne when I suddenly felt my bowels doing a light fandango. I excused myself and went to the bathroom. I felt as though I were about to have diarrhea. I sat for a few minutes but nothing happened. I began to feel worse, light-headed and both warm and cold at the same time. Maybe I needed to throw up. I kneeled over the bowl, but again nothing happened. I was now extremely hot and began to feel dizzy. The cold floor tiles looked inviting. I lay down with my face against the tiles. I was chilled and completely enervated, but those tiles felt so good. If I could just lie there a moment . . .

Suzanne was banging on the door and calling my name. She tried to push the door open, but I was lying in the way. "What's wrong? Are you all right?" she asked, alarm in her voice.

"I'm okay," I said, shifting slightly so she could open the door some. "I felt woozy."

"I got worried," she said. "You've been in here at least fifteen minutes. I thought something had happened."

I lumbered to my feet and told her what I'd experienced. I felt much better now. I drank a couple of glasses of water and joined them in the living room. Sally said it sounded as though I'd had an anxiety attack. I had no idea myself; I hadn't been thinking about anything in particular before the feeling came over me. Maybe the day's events had simply caught up with me.

We said goodnight to Sally and went upstairs. I intended to go down again after Suzanne had gone to sleep. She got into bed and told me she didn't think she could make it. The pain was too great. She was feeling terrible. She was as low as I'd seen her. I tried to be comforting. I told her that we had now gotten through two days. Tomorrow we'd get through a third, the day after a fourth, and so on. We just had to take it one day at a time and soon we'd discover that a lot of days had passed. Before we realized it was happening, we would begin to feel better. In this case, time was on our side.

"Think of other times when you've really been hurt," I said. "You know that the passage of time made a difference."

"But this is different," she said.

"It's different in that it's the greatest possible hurt, the worst kind," I replied, "but even this will get better." Maybe if I could convince her, I could convince myself.

"Listen," I said, "we've suffered the worst kind of death there is. It's beyond words to describe the horror we're undergoing. But others have endured it. Look at Sally. When she lost Jeb, she was alone. Yet she survived. Sure, she hasn't gotten over it; one doesn't *get over* the death of a child. But she gets pleasure out of living, even though the pain is there. She told you that. And she was alone. We, at least, have each other."

"I know," she answered, "but it hurts. It hurts so much." The pain in her voice was terrible.

"We owe it to Peter not to crack," I told her. "It would make his death even more meaningless than it was. And understand this, Lovey. Right now you're feeling as low as you're getting to feel. You're in a trough. You're in the bottom of the valley. You may never get to the peak again, but you'll get part way up the mountain at least. You know that it's a question of peaks and valleys, highs and lows." She didn't say anything, so I continued, "You're always saying that's part of my problem; I can't seem to find a middle ground; I'm either up or down. Well, right now you're in a low, and you know that they never last. All you can do is tell yourself that no matter how bad you feel right now, it will get better. You *know* it will. Take comfort in that knowledge."

"You're right, I know," she said, "but I don't think I can take the lows."

"The hell you can't," I snapped. "You're a strong person, Suzanne. Look at how well you've done up to now. Look how well you've been functioning. You've been giving help and comfort to other people, especially to the kids. Don't tell me you can't take it. And remember what Doris told you earlier, that you could handle anything life had to deal you if you could handle this, that this was the worst. She wasn't holding that out to you as an abstract possibility. She meant it in the sense that you *are* handling this. Just hang on to the thought that you're strong, and that no matter how bad you feel at any particular point, it will get better. Forget that it's a cliché; time does help."

She squeezed my hand and turned onto her side. I continued to sit on the edge of the bed until her breathing took on a deeper, more regular rhythm. Then I got up quietly and went downstairs.

I made myself a cup of tea and sat in the living room. I got a notepad because I wanted to list some of the things that needed to be done the next morning. I had discovered by this point that lists or notes were essential. Although I felt I was in fairly good shape, I realized that my mind wasn't as responsive as I was accustomed to its being. Points, both important and trivial, would flit in and out haphazardly, not subject to my control. To combat this phenomenon, I started making notes as points occurred to me.

Off and on throughout the day, I had wrestled with the idea of doing something at Peter's service. I felt I had to do something other than simply be there; I had to take some small part in the proceedings. But what to do? Almost without intending it, I began to see the outline of a poem forming in my mind. For the past two days I had had a sense of inevitability about Peter's death, as though all the decisions we had made in the course of our marriage that eventually led to our moving to Connecticut, and all the traits in Peter's character—both hereditary and acquired—that made him what he was, led inexorably to that moment on the road. In that sense, he had a rendezvous. I don't mean I believed his death was predestined, for that would imply a Predestinator, an entity I don't believe in. But I couldn't shake this idea of his having a dark rendezvous.

With that theme in mind, I found lines quickly forming themselves. I don't suppose I spent more than half an hour on it. From the beginning, though, I knew that I was writing it to read at the service. I felt it was something I had to do for Peter. But the thought was frightening. To get up before all those people feeling the way I would be feeling and read this . . . I looked at the poem again. Jesus, to read this . . . trash! I worked on it some more, changing a word here or there, but it remained essentially the same poem. I tried a different tack; it went nowhere. I was stuck with what I had. Perhaps I could read an appropriate poem by a real poet. I started toward the bookcase, but sopped myself. *"You chickenshit bastard,"* I thought. *"You can't even do this for the kid."* I tongue-lashed myself a little longer before I realized I could read the poem to Sally Bowers in the morning to see what she thought. It was a comforting idea. I turned off the lights and went up to bed.

In bed, images from the day and lines from the poem flashed through my mind. I would read the poem tomorrow . . . Peter's gone . . . Peter's out of it . . . why should I keep on living, keep on striving? Because I owe it to Peter? Not sure . . . not sure I owe him anything . . . maybe I do and maybe I don't . . . He's no more . . . gone . . . in a body in a box . . . He was but he isn't . . . I am but must sleep . . . escape . . . hide in lavender dress . . . hide in Suzanne . . . crawl inside and die and be born again without memory . . . without pain.

Friday was another scorcher, the air heavy and moist. I went down to the kitchen where Sally Bowers was making coffee. She said Suzanne had left a note saying she was taking a walk. I felt this was a good sign. For some time, Suzanne had been on a happiness-through-health campaign, which involved a three-to-four-mile walk-jog early each morning. I was pleased that she had returned to her regimen.

I told Sally I wanted her to listen to a poem I had written and judge its suitability for the service. After I read it to her, I expressed my misgivings; namely, I had doubts about its quality as well as my own motivation. Was I doing this for Peter or for myself? She smiled and told me I really should try to be a little less critically self-analytical. "It's not one of your most charming characteristics," she said. She declared that the poem was certainly appropriate and that I should read it. "Whom you're writing it for is irrelevant; you're writing it for both of you," she pointed out. She suggested I check with Suzanne, who had just returned.

Suzanne had enjoyed her walk, although it had not been an entirely pleasant experience. This was the first time she had really been alone, and it had felt good. She had been quite self-conscious, however; she had felt as though everyone, people driving past and people inside their houses, were watching her. They must have been saying, "There's the mother who lost her child." It was an uncomfortable feeling. She was also conscious that the last mile or so had been a retracing of Peter's route that night. This hadn't been deliberate on her part; it was the usual course we took. In fact, given the geography of the area, it was unavoidable. I told her I had experienced a similar feeling when I'd returned from the florist yesterday. As I'd passed the reservoir I had thought, *"He had five minutes left to live at this point";* at a four-way stop sign, *"about three minutes left";* branching onto our road, *"just about a minute now."* As I'd approached the pole, I'd been thinking, *"This is ghoulish, morbid. What's wrong with me? Now he's hit the curb, he's flipping through the air."* I'd passed the pole with no sense of climax, no tears, no anger. I'd been numb, emotionally empty. I'd sat in the car a moment before going into the house.

A grisly thing had happened on her walk, Suzanne said. An Alsatian she had never seen before had joined her near the scene of the accident. When it had gotten near the pole, it had started sniffing and pawing around, its ears laid back. It had moved to the bloody area, which really excited its interest. This had been too much for Suzanne. With a combination of entreaties and threats,

64

she had driven the dog off. She couldn't have just walked away, letting the dog maul the area, she said.

I read her the poem, saying that if she had no objections, I'd read it at the service. She had me read it twice. She held me and said tearfully that I should read it. "I'm just glad you didn't spring it on me at the church," she said.

We left a little before ten to meet Dale at the funeral home. Big Peter and a couple of the Mitchells were there. While Suzanne talked with them inside, I smoked some cigarettes outside on a shaded porch and waited for Dale. About the only thing that had given me any pleasure the last couple of days were cigarettes. Someone, I forget whom, had said yesterday, "Are you using those again?" He had clearly been disturbed by my return to tobacco. "Yeah," I had said, "I'm really worried about lung cancer right now." That had shut him up. As I stood waiting, I mulled over the irony that something so patently harmful as tobacco should also be so damnably pleasurable. When my thoughts turned to the self-destructive nature of tobacco addiction, I started counting the passing cars. I saw Dale drive in, and, putting out my cigarette, I walked over to meet him.

We went inside and I introduced Dale. He and Suzanne and I then went to see Peter. We stood a while, at first silent, then making desultory conversation. Some other people came in. After a bit, Dale sat down in a row of folding chairs along the inner wall. He looked so utterly forlorn, so distressed, that I walked over and sat down beside him. We sat for a long time before Dale moved back to the casket. He asked if he could be alone with Peter for a few minutes. After he came out, Suzanne went in alone for her final goodbye. A symbolic gesture really, for she is still saying goodbye.

The undertaker gave Suzanne Peter's ring, which she in turn gave to Big Peter who in turn gave it to his nephew, Tony. It turned out that Peter's two grandmothers had had an animated discussion the day before while standing by the casket. They both felt the gold ring should be removed because the people at the crematorium would surely steal it. It would be foolish to leave it on his finger. Suzanne had overheard the conversation and, although offended by it, recognized that they were probably right. She had asked the undertaker to remove it after everyone had left that night. He could give it to her Friday. At first I was hurt, then angry, but quickly understood the truth of their position. As a self-proclaimed cynic, I should have realized that no area of mortal experience is exempt from human cupidity. The practical, everyday world was reasserting itself, intruding into our grief.

We went home, Suzanne riding with Dale. We found that preparations were in full swing. More food had arrived, and Doris had bought two tubs in which to put ice and beer and soda. She figured we would have a number of people coming over after the service. Suzanne and Dale had lunch, Dale making one of the most enormous sandwiches I've ever seen. I think he had a little of everything in the house in it. Afterward, he went up to Peter's room to sit by himself a while.

Suzanne had lain down for a rest by the time the Episcopal minister, Bob Tate, arrived. He and Dale and I had coffee while we discussed the service. Suzanne had said that she wanted the Twenty-third Psalm read, but other than that I left it to the two clergymen to choose the passages. They decided that Bob would read most of the liturgy and Dale would deliver a eulogy. I had told Big Peter earlier of my intention to read a poem, and asked him if he wished to read or say anything. He'd decided he'd rather not. I'd said my reading could be for the two of us.

I asked Bob if I could have a glass of water handy at the altar, perhaps hidden behind some flowers, as my throat and mouth tended to go dry under the slightest tension. Even in the classroom I always had a mug of coffee close at hand. More important, however, I was worried that the emotion of the moment might overcome me so I wouldn't be able to continue. Bob reassured me by saying that if that happened, I should glance at him, and he would come over and finish reading the poem himself. After he and Dale had run through the service again, Bob left to make sure everything was in readiness at the church and to make copies of the song we intended to have sung.

Barbara, another of our neighbors, planned to stay in our house during the service. She said that one of the favorite tricks of thieves was to read the death notices in the newspaper to find out when funeral services were being held—often a guarantee of an empty house. She asked where the vacuum was. I tried to object, but Doris told me to shut up and get dressed. There wasn't much time before the service was to begin.

5

BY THREE-THIRTY, the house was nearly bursting with relatives and old friends. This was good because it kept us too busy to worry about the services. There was something about the official, ritualized formality of a church service that was dreadful. I suppose it was just one more piece of business that brought home to me the irrefutable fact of Peter's death. I knew damn well, of course, that he was dead, but the idea was so abhorrent that I kept rejecting it—or trying to reject it. Each step in the ritual process thus became threatening, because it prevented me from hiding from the harsh reality. Each step was a proclamation that rang out the words "Your son is dead." Necessary, I suppose, but painful.

I had another reason for wanting people around. I felt that something momentous had happened—as indeed it had—something I had to share with others, just as if I'd become engaged or inherited a million dollars. It was too important to keep to myself. Something had happened that would profoundly affect, if not change, my life.

Big Peter arrived to drive Suzanne and me to the church. Before we left, he spent a few minutes in Peter's room. Suzanne told him how apprehensive she was about the service. He put his arms around her comfortingly and reassured her.

There were a lot of cars in the church parking lot. The Episcopal church is part of a complex that also houses a Presbyterian church. I figured there must be a function at the Presbyterian church as well. We parked and walked to the church. The weather was still miserable, and the atmosphere enveloped us like a warm, moist cloak, making movement sluggish and unpleasant. I hoped the building was air-conditioned.

Other people were also arriving. At the door were several members of my group just entering. One of them, Linda, stopped, and we embraced briefly. We didn't exchange a word, but her pain and warmth emanated from her, completely enfolding me. It was the most perfect expression of feeling I have ever encountered, stunning in its impact.

Coral and Tammy were standing on either side of the door, handing a daisy to everyone who entered. Tammy was substituting for Clista, who was on her way from work. We entered. The church was roughly fan-shaped, with the chancel at the narrow end and the nave spread out before it. The altar was plain and bare. A large arrangement of yellow and brown flowers on the wall behind it was the only decoration. The pews were formed into six sections, separated by aisles. The only empty pews were the two front ones in the center sections. That meant about four hundred people were there. I was staggered. Who were they all? As we walked down the center aisle, I became aware that people were looking at us. The bereaved parents. Christ! I felt my heart thumping in my chest, shattering my brief period of tranquility. My mouth was so dry I couldn't swallow. I ran my tongue over the roof of my mouth; it was like licking cardboard.

I noticed more people entering, pushing into the already crowded pews. I took this opportunity to nip into the sacristy for a drink of water. Bob and Dale were there, Bob changing into his vestments. I reminded them about the glass of water and returned to my seat, threading my way through people who were milling around, looking for a place to sit. I saw that Suzanne's mother, Sally and Gardiner, Dr. and Mrs. Mitchell, and some other family members were now seated in our section. Off to one side, a young man was softly strumming a guitar. Given Peter's love of rock music, we had felt it would be inappropriate, as well as needlessly painful, to have an organ cranking out doleful airs. We didn't need any external stimuli to put us into a mournful mood. I had said to Suzanne, who believes in an afterlife, that Peter would never forgive us.

The guitarist finished playing, and the church was still except for occasional coughing or nose-blowing. We all stood. From the back of the church, I heard Bob's and Dale's voices as they alternately recited the opening passages of The Burial of the Dead. Each moved slowly down a separate aisle until they came together in front of the altar. When they had finished, Bob said a few more prayers, including one especially intended for the death of a child. He then led us in a recitation of the Twenty-third

Psalm, after which we sat down, and Dale offered a brief homily.

He remarked that Peter had been a fortunate young man, twice-blessed in that he had not only a mother but also two fathers. Two fathers whom he loved and who loved him. Dale indicated that this was not simply empty rhetoric suitable to the occasion, but a conviction that Peter had honestly held. And he should know.

As Dale was speaking, I felt in the left side of my chest a powerful, constrictive pressure which quickly turned to sharp, jabbing pain. I was sure that I was going into cardiac arrest. For the past three days I had felt quite certain that I didn't care if I lived or died. Sometimes I had wished I would die, convinced that death would bring an end to suffering. Each of the past two nights part of me had hoped that I wouldn't wake the next morning. But, when I experienced that chest pain, my immediate, instinctive reaction was, *"No, no. I don't want to die yet—and not here."* Certainly not here. I have never cared for melodramatics, and the thought of expiring during Peter's service was a piece of upstaging I could do without. I made myself relax and breathe slowly and concentrate on what Dale was saying.

It was clear that Dale was almost finished, and I knew that I was up next. I started to become anxious, fearful of the task ahead. Questions flew through my head. Was I worried about flubbing it for Peter's sake or for that of my own elephantine ego? How much of what I was going through was real and how much was a performance by the poor bereaved parent? Was I doing it as a tribute to Peter or for myself? Always the self-doubts. In my mind, I could hear Sally Bowers telling me to shape up.

Dale ended by saying, "Ben will now read his poem." I found that possessive pronoun disturbing, as though it gave an emphasis I didn't want: *Ben will now lay his egg.* Maybe that was it: I wanted to be dissociated from it. But I don't think so. I felt it was more a case of this being Peter's poem, not mine. It was my gift to him. It shouldn't be called *my* poem.

I walked to the altar and noticed the glass of water, which Coral had placed there earlier, sitting on the nearly empty altar, a shining beacon of my insecurity. I turned to face the congregation and was stunned at the number of people. The entire concave wall at the back of the church was lined with people standing. The face of an ex-colleague, Brian, leaped out at me. Brian was at Middlebury that summer, and I thought, *"My God, he's come all the way down for us."* The double doors behind the center aisle were open, and I saw a crowd of people packed in the vestibule. I didn't think we knew that many people who cared enough to subject themselves to this ordeal. I was also struck by the number of youngsters. I had the impression that at least half of those present were teenagers.

I began to read. It isn't very good poetry, but it does capture certain aspects of Peter's character as well as express my sense of his dark rendezvous:

I wish my son that you had not gone;
I wish my son that you could have stayed;
I wish you were home in bed asleep;
But the night was dark
        And you had a rendezvous to keep.

You wanted to walk before you could stand;
Then you wanted to run before you could walk;
You were never afraid of the daring leap;
But the night was dark
      And you had a rendezvous to keep.

I know that your yearnings were incredibly strong;
That your wants and your needs were uniquely your own;
And your feelings were real and honest and deep;
But the night was dark
      And you had a rendezvous to keep.

I love you my son for all that you were;
I love you my son for all that you weren't;
But I am consoled and I shall not weep;
Even though the night was dark
      And you had a rendezvous to keep.

    As I returned to my seat, Bob began playing the opening bars of "Blowin' in the Wind," which we then sang. For me, it was the most difficult and most moving part of the service. We had selected it because it was one piece of music that held special meaning for the three of us. It harked back to a period when we almost always did things as a family unit. Two of our undertakings were involvement in the antiwar and the civil-rights movements, and, of course, Dylan and his music were associated with them. Dylan, in fact, was one of the few musicians in whom Peter and we shared an interest. Also, "Blowin' in the Wind" struck a couple of themes pertinent to us.

    The opening lines, which ask, in effect, what a person

must do to be called a man, express a concern that I knew Peter felt very strongly. His desire to be treated as his own person, to be considered a man, was one of his motivating drives. As I tried to indicate in the poem, he had always been impatient for the next stage in his development to begin. So the question in these lines was one that, figuratively, he had been asking of late. Although a source of conflict between us, that characteristic of Peter's was one which I had understood and with which I had sympathized, so Dylan's words were quite appropriate for us.

Two other lines, which raise the question of an individual's social and political responsibilities, suggest an attitude we tried to instill in Peter. Although it sounds rather pompous when put badly, we wanted to teach him through our words and actions to stand up for what he believed, to oppose injustice and bigotry, and to face the truth as he perceived it. He wasn't to put blinders on himself, as so many did. To a large extent, I know that we were successful.

After the song, Dale rose to deliver the eulogy. He was dressed in a dark suit, and he paced back and forth as he spoke. I don't remember very much of it. Although I tried to pay attention, my mind kept wandering. In those early days I found it difficult to focus on what other people were saying.

Dale began by speaking to our five-year-old nephew Tommy (by way of Suzanne's brother Tom), who had been crying intermittently throughout the service. He told him to be comforted, that he understood he had lost his only male cousin, and that he knew how much he had admired Peter. He recalled seeing Tommy try to lift Peter's weights in his room earlier that day, but they had been too heavy for him. He told him that as he got bigger, he could begin to do some of the things that Peter had done.

Most of the time Dale spoke as though he were talking directly to Peter. He said how shocked he had been to hear of Peter's death, but not surprised, because Peter had always pushed dangerously close to the limits. He spoke of his love for Peter and also of his anger. He said he could kick him in the rear end for buying that moped. He spoke of Peter's wonderfully expressive brown eyes and his engaging smile, of his warmth and attractiveness. He said that Peter had a considerable amount of natural charm, which had certainly captured him. Peter had slipped through his defenses and moved him; he had been touched by Peter.

Dale mentioned one point that surprised me. He said Peter had lacked self-confidence with girls, that he had had no idea how attractive he was. I'd had no idea Peter felt that way; in fact, I'd assumed quite the opposite. He'd had two serious girlfriends, and many others would stop by the house or phone. I had actually been a bit jealous at what I felt was his obvious success, so I was really astonished to learn of his insecurity.

One thing that didn't surprise me was Dale's recounting of the first time Peter had gone to him professionally. He had walked into Dale's office and said, "Hey, shrink, what can you do for me?" Knowing Dale, I'm sure he'd responded, "Well, what would you like me to do for you?" Of course, Peter had known Dale before, but it was just the kind of brash remark Peter would make.

That's all I remember clearly, although I recall he

spoke of Peter's dislike of hypocrisy, his confusion that people couldn't be "authentic." He said Peter had possessed *joie de vivre* and the ability to feel for others, and he had been basically hopeful about himself and about life. Dale ended by asking people to place their daisies on the altar as they left.

His words were scarcely out of his mouth when little Tommy raced up to the altar with his daisy. I believe I heard a parental gasp from his pew as he did so, but, to me, it was a fitting ending. The child is dead; long live the child.

We took our flowers to the altar and went outside, where the wet heat embraced us. We began thanking people for attending. We were soon engulfed in the mob of exiting mourners. It was a poignant moment, as people either expressed their own sorrow or extended their sympathy to us in ours. My memory is again vague, but a few vignettes stand out. A King parent rushed by me in obvious distress, saying she couldn't talk now. An ex-student of mine shook my hand silently while a tear slowly trickled down his cheek. Someone wanted to know what was going to be done with all the flowers. I told him they were to go to a nursing home in Norwalk.

A group of kids from Stamford Catholic stood off to one side, looking confused and uncomfortable. Mike, Peter's best friend at Stamford Catholic, had seen to it that all Peter's friends at the school had been notified. Each had written a short message to Peter and wrapped it around a red rose. Mike told me later that they selected the rose because it was the symbol of the Grateful Dead, Peter's favorite rock group. I introduced myself to each of the kids and thanked them. I noticed a few minutes later that Suzanne was embracing each one as well.

I could think of nothing appropriate to say to people except to thank them for coming, yet it seemed incongruous to me. It was as though I were saying thank you for suffering, thank you for being as lost and confused and helpless as I am. I realized, of course, that I was thanking them for caring, but my words still sounded awkward to me. I realized, too, how hard it must be for our other relatives and for Peter's friends. Virtually all the attention was given to us the parents. Everyone expressed concern for us, while others who were extremely close to him were ignored. No one asked them how they were doing.

Many people, a number of whom I didn't know, said it was a beautiful and moving service. That made me feel good. We had sent the kid off in fine style.

Soon, nearly everyone had departed. I noticed Frank sitting on a low wall by the church entrance. He looked so alone, so bereft, that it was heartbreaking. I went over and spoke to him. He said the kids were going to get some beer and go to a local park. He was going with them. I told him to be careful. He said he would be. Kids always say that.

By the time we got home, a great crowd had already assembled. I moved about, talking with people, accepting their condolences, feeling their pain. I made my way inside to get some coffee, pushing through the line waiting at the buffet. Doris was too busy to notice me scuttling past with just coffee. The heat had begun to diminish, but the house was still hot and stuffy and unpleasant. It began to close in on me. I went outside again.

I wasn't having a very good time. People kept speaking to me, but their words weren't making much sense. I joined a small group, hoping to blend in and not have to talk myself. They were talking about some of their teenage escapades, the point being how capricious life is. At the moment there was only one teenage escapade of any interest to me, so I moved off.

I saw an old family friend, Julian, talking with Suzanne. He was saying that during the service he'd looked around the church and had been amazed to see that people of all ages seemed to be feeling a deep, personal loss. He remarked that the number of kids present was a compliment to Peter. I couldn't argue with that. As Peter had had a strong zest for living and had responded to people as individuals rather than as stereotypes, it shouldn't have surprised us that there was a large turnout. I don't know how many enemies he may have had, but he sure as hell had a lot of friends.

I made a few more attempts at conversation, but they weren't much use. My heart wasn't in it. People seemed to be strangers to me. I felt no sense of connection with them. I felt little connection with anything about them.

Time was passing and the crowd began thinning. I got more coffee and sat outside again. A young woman was sitting on the grass near me. As she rose, her dress rode up, exposing a fair amount of leg. Very nice leg. I felt a tiny flutter in my loins and realized I hadn't had a sexual thought in three days. Almost before I knew it, my mind had moved from legs to pudendum to penetration to climax to fertilization to birth to death to Peter. The fluttering stopped.

By six-thirty I was beat. As I said goodbye to my niece

and nephew, I realized I had had it; I was near collapse. I sensed depression coming on and knew I had to get away. I was feeling terrible about Peter and didn't want to speak to another soul. I located Suzanne and told her I was going to bed. A couple of people were in the process of getting drunk, which was annoying Suzanne. It seemed inappropriate to her. She realized that they weren't simply using this as an excuse for a party, that they were coping in their own way. Nonetheless, it was upsetting.

I told her there was nothing I could do about it; I couldn't speak to another person. I went upstairs, barely able to move. I understood that another part of the mourning process was completed, but that didn't hold much meaning for me. I had just gotten into bed when Suzanne came up. She rubbed my head and gave me a pep talk, much along the lines of the one I'd given her a night or two before. I was asleep before she left the room.

I awoke about ten when Suzanne came to bed. I couldn't get back to sleep and soon realized I was ravenously hungry. I went downstairs thinking of all the goodies I had seen earlier but had had no appetite for at the time. I remembered thinking then that the table would collapse from the load. But I quickly discovered that there was scarcely a scrap left; we had been picked clean. I had some tea and toast and went back to bed.

C H A P T E R

6

BABS ARRIVED Saturday. Although we had talked to her on the phone, I knew that her visit would be a painful one for her and for us. She was closer to Peter than most of our adult friends. We had shared a house for a year, and her oldest son, Frank, as I've said, had been one of Peter's closest friends. I also suspected that when she entered our house, with its atmosphere of sorrow, all the old pain associated with the elder Frank's death would tear at her. I know it did with me. I had been thinking of her husband a lot since Peter died, wishing, for example, that he could have conducted Peter's service, for he had been not just a friend but an Episcopal priest.

But it was as a friend that I missed him. I missed his strength and his compassion and his good humor. He could not have changed the harsh reality of Peter's death, but he could have made living with it more bearable. He had had an almost infinite capacity for helping others.

The terrible irony is that he couldn't help himself, or find help, when he most needed it. I had been with him the morning of the day he had killed himself and had had absolutely no inkling of how desperate he was. I have relived that morning countless times, vainly searching for clues that should have alerted me to his state of despondency.

We had a good chat with Babs, reminiscing at times and looking fruitlessly to the future at others. It was the kind of desultory conversation old friends have when they realize that words are less important than companionship. Sally Bowers had lunch with Babs and Suzanne before she left. I couldn't help marveling at the accumulated pain represented at the table. I'm sure each of them was thinking along similar lines. It was sad to have Sally Bowers leave, but she had business to attend to, and she had been with us when we most needed her. There's no way to measure these things, of course, but her presence helped us survive. Her function was similar to that of the tribal scapegoat who assumes the sins of others for the welfare of the community. Only in this case it was pain and not sin that required expiation.

Babs spent the night, and the next afternoon she and her son drove home. Suzanne and I sat in the living room looking at one another, alone for the first time since that Wednesday morning. It was something we would have to get used to, and it wasn't very pleasant.

Jane and Michael took us out to dinner Sunday night. We had decided, tacitly, that we would resume the daily semblance of life. To go out to dinner or not didn't really matter. Peter was dead either way. We had a nice time, and it helped take us out of ourselves. It also helped take my mind off a disagreeable task we faced the next day.

On Monday Suzanne and I drove to Long Island to see my mother, who was hospitalized with a broken hip. She was supposed to have visited us the previous Friday, but her hip had prevented that. She was, in effect, isolated, and had spoken to no one except my Aunt Grace and my sister, neither of whom had given her any indication about Phoebe, or later, Peter. In fact, my sister was to have seen her that Sunday, but postponed her visit until after I had broken the news. Before Peter died, we had decided not to tell her about Phoebe until she came up, because she was very fond of dogs. And I certainly wasn't going to tell someone in her condition about Peter over the telephone.

Mother is an intelligent, cultured, and sensitive woman, with little use for theatrics. She had been suffering hallucinations in the hospital because of one of the medicines she was receiving. She'd also experienced two rather extraordinary psychic episodes. In order to make sense of Mother's first premonition, I need to drag Sir Benjamin onto the scene.

Rapparee Sir Benjamin Bullseye was Phoebe's replacement. After Phoebe died, Suzanne and Peter and I had decided we would get another bull terrier. Although I'd been opposed to getting Phoebe, she had quickly won me over, so I was as keen as they to obtain another bull terrier. Suzanne had located a breeder who had some puppies, so within a few days of Phoebe's death we brought home the seven-week-old Sir Benjamin. He was quite a mess. Two weeks before, he and two litter mates had gotten into a fierce brawl. The three of them had to be taken to the vet's for treatment, including antibiotics. He lost the tip of his right ear and had several nasty bites. Even so, he was a cute little guy, white like Phoebe, but with a black eye. Peter, the chauvinist, had wanted a male in the first place (they run about ten pounds heavier than the females), so when he had come home from work and found Sir Benjamin, he had been elated.

Mother had told me on the phone the last time we'd spoken how pleased she was that Suzanne had brought Phoebe's puppy for her to see. That was four days after we'd gotten Sir Benjamin and three days before Peter had died. It took me a while to convince her that Suzanne had not been to visit her. Furthermore, I'd said that no hospital would allow a dog inside. Aside from the fact that Sir Benjamin was not technically Phoebe's puppy, it was a remarkable coincidence.

Even more startling was her other experience. She was asleep when we arrived that Monday. After she awoke fully and recognized Suzanne and me, she said, "Oh, Ben, you're all right."

"Yes, Mother," I said, "but we have some bad news for you." I took her hand.

"Hank? Has something happened to Hank?" she asked, referring to my older brother.

"No, Hank's okay. He's on his way home from Kuwait, but he's not here yet. It's Peter, Mother. He was killed in an accident a few days ago."

"Oh, dear God!" she exclaimed softly and fell back on her pillows. She was holding my hand tightly. Although there were tears in her eyes, she seemed almost relieved. "I knew . . . I just knew something was wrong, but no one would tell me anything."

At this point the head nurse came in to see if Mother

needed assistance. On our way in, we had told her the purpose of our visit and asked that she be handy in case the news was too much for Mother. But Mother was coping.

Suzanne and Mother spoke together for a few minutes, and then Mother told us what she had experienced. Because of her hallucinatory state, she still had difficulty separating fact from fancy. She said that Suzanne had been to see her and she had looked terrible. Her eyes had been red and swollen, and she had appeared very sad. Mother had known something appalling had happened, but Suzanne wouldn't speak. She hadn't said a word; she'd just sat there looking wretched. And then she had gone. The remarkable point is that in a sense Suzanne had refused to speak to Mother because of our decision not to tell her immediately about Peter.

So powerful was the influence of this incident upon Mother that it took us some time to persuade her that Suzanne had not visited her. Mother said that she had had a premonition that something had happened to Hank or me or Peter, but that she suspected it was Hank. The doctors and nurses had told her she was simply feeling the side effects of the medicine. She had even begged Aunt Grace to tell her the truth. Aunt Grace, who has no capacity for lying, managed to soothe her by swearing that Hank was fine so far as she knew.

I used the word *premonition*, but, strictly speaking, these weren't premonitions because they were not forewarnings of events yet to happen, but a kind of telepathic knowledge of events that had already occurred.

Mother was relieved, in fact, when we told her, for now she at least knew the truth. As horrible as that truth was, she knew that Hank and I were safe. She said it had been ghastly, confined to bed *knowing* something was wrong, and everyone telling her to take it easy. She had had these premonitions a few other times in her life, and they had always turned out to be correct. Understandably, she dreaded them.

Before we left, I told her I'd call the next day to reassure her that we had visited her, in case she should come to think that our visit was a hallucination as well. I make no pretense of understanding Mother's experiences or the nature of the phenomena involved. She didn't have all the facts straight, but she certainly apprehended the spirit of the events.

Two days later my brother and his family arrived home on Long Island. They had been delayed because they had stopped in Europe to visit some relatives. He phoned to let me know he was home and to find out where Mother was. He hadn't spoken to anyone else yet, so he didn't know about Peter. I told him. It was brutal. Hank was so flushed with the excitement of homecoming that my news hit him doubly hard. It was as if our conversation had gone: "Hi, Ben. I'm home." "Hi, Hank. Peter's dead." The next day he came up.

Hank is eight years older than I, with two young sons to whom he's completely devoted. He also was very fond of Peter, and always brought him something when he returned from abroad. When Peter was about five, Hank had given him a python skin he had gotten in Indonesia. Peter had taken it on the television show "Wonderama" and won the show-and-tell competition. It had been amusing to watch him struggle with the ten-foot snakeskin. The show's host had finally held one end and Peter

85

the other as the youthful audience shrieked and yelled its approval. His prize had been a first-class sleeping bag, which he used for years.

Suzanne and I made it a point to cover as completely as we could all the details of Peter's death, including the service, even to taking him to the place of the accident. At first he was reluctant, but we explained that we thought it would be helpful for him. It was clear to us that he was devastated by the event, and, since he had been absent at the time, we wanted to share with him what we had been undergoing. In this way, we hoped, Peter's death would be more real to him, and he would be better able to deal with it. We were conscious, especially because of Mother, how terrible it is for someone to be left out in a circumstance of such deep emotional intensity as this. As it was, Hank was having difficulty accepting the fact of Peter's death. We could see that he was struggling to believe the unbelievable. We knew the feeling well.

In the days since Peter's service, people continued to drop by or phone (and many sent letters of condolence or Mass cards). I had a sense of two events. The first was Peter's death. The second was the outflowing of love and warmth and sympathy we received from others. The second didn't touch the first; it made no difference in our suffering over Peter, but it did give us something else, something additional, something valuable. It helped sustain us when our pain was at its lacerating worst.

Occasionally, however, a sour note would sound in the symphony of compassion that was being played for us. A few days after Peter died, Thurman Munson, the Yankee catcher, was killed in a plane crash. Someone who apparently knew that Peter was a Yankee fan said perhaps

Peter and Thurman were having a catch somewhere. That was *so* sweet, *so* lovely, I felt like dispatching that individual so he could have a catch with them too. Dealing with Peter's death was difficult enough without people dripping sentimentality over me. I felt that comments of that sort demeaned my grief, reduced it to soap-opera proportions. The kid and the catcher on the Big Diamond in the Sky. I felt murderous.

Suzanne returned to work on August 6th, eight working days after Peter died. Personnel policy at the health department allowed five days' bereavement leave for members of the immediate family. Including weekends, Suzanne had had about a week and a half off, but she found that time totally inadequate to prepare her for returning to her job. She dreaded the return, but we agreed she had to do it sometime.

Her most compelling reason for not wanting to return was her desire to remain in the safety and security of home. She didn't want to face the curious eyes that would be examining her for traces of her ordeal. Actually, she looked surprisingly good, except for a slightly drawn countenance and some puffiness around the eyes, but it wasn't her own looks that worried her so much as the looks of others. She would be an object of curiosity.

For several days, Suzanne had been steeling herself emotionally to go back. After the initial shock had passed, her feelings began to open like spring buds, exposing her to the harsh winds of our new reality. She had begun to cry, usually for brief periods, but these periods would occur many times throughout the day. She told herself that her crying and depression were normal under the circumstances. If others at work couldn't handle her grief, that was their problem. Still, it wasn't pleasant to contemplate.

As it turned out, most people were warm and kind and supportive, so much so that Suzanne spent most of the first day in tears, joined at times by various of her associates. The health department had closed the afternoon of Peter's service, and most of the employees had attended. Thus, Suzanne was among people who really hurt for her, which made it easier in the sense that her colleagues did not erect that wall of unspoken embarrassment and awkwardness which so often greets the returning mourner. Also, Peter had often popped by to see her for one reason or another, so many of her co-workers had gotten to know him. Not just know, but like, because Peter could be very friendly and charming. So it was to an almost familial atmosphere that Suzanne returned.

At first, she was completely unproductive. She couldn't concentrate, nor could she pick up the threads from projects she had been working on prior to Peter's death. She began to make lists of what she wanted to accomplish, annotating her calendar in greater detail, and clearing her desk of trivial matters. She wanted to be as organized as possible, for she had only the one week before we went out West to bury Peter's ashes in the family plot in Colorado Springs.

We had been busy organizing and settling Peter's affairs as well. He had been insured on a family policy for a thousand dollars. The salesman had advised it, saying that Peter could get much lower premiums this way when he converted as an adult. A thousand dollars. When the check arrived, I held it in my hand, weighing it. It felt so light. A thousand dollars for Peter. That came out to a little under sixteen cents a day for each day of his life. I seemed to be obsessed with illogical and erratic details like that. I had an urge to tear the check in shreds, but handed it to Suzanne instead. I went outside and mowed the lawn.

Suzanne had been puttering around in Peter's room one day and came across a receipt for a safe-deposit box. It was the first we had known of it. We checked with the bank, and, sure enough, Peter had a box there. We would have to produce his key, as the bank had no duplicates, and, of course, we would need official authorization to open the box. More red tape. Thus began the Great Search.

We went through his room quite thoroughly, but we couldn't find it. We asked Coral and a few of his other friends. A couple of them knew about the box, but didn't know where he kept—translation: hid—the key. I went through his room again, as well as the attic, the basement, and the garage. No luck. The bank informed us it would cost between sixty and seventy dollars to have a locksmith open it. Further, the locksmith couldn't get to it at once, so we'd have to wait until we returned from Colorado. That meant several weeks of anxiety, because we could think of only one good reason why he would have a safe-deposit box. Dope. What an ugly postscript that would be. Our imaginations ran wild envisioning what we would find.

Another unpleasant experience was dealing with the friendly folks at Social Security. They were real sweethearts. Since Peter had worked, he was entitled to Social Security death benefits, and we had filed the necessary papers with Social Security. Big Peter paid the funeral home, and we reimbursed him for our share. Apparently, Social Security must either send the check to the funeral home, or, if the bill has been paid, to the person who paid it. This point had not been made clear to us, and when we inquired about the check, we were treated as though we were trying to defraud either Big Peter or Social Security itself. Their rudeness and mean-mindedness was a reminder that the world was going about its business as usual, unaffected by our personal tragedy. After all the sympathy and kindness we had been receiving, this treatment was all the more startling.

The one pleasant undertaking we had while tying up loose ends was closing Peter's savings account. The people at the bank were very sympathetic and helpful. They told us precisely what the law required us to do and how best to do it. They went out of their way to be cooperative. It was nice to deal with people who didn't give the impression that we were interrupting their coffee break.

A final piece of business before us was getting rid of the moped. The night of the accident it had been taken to a local garage. We weren't able to make satisfactory arrangements with the garage for them to sell it, so we drove down to pick it up. I was caught off guard by my reaction. As I lifted it into the back of our station wagon, I felt as though I'd touched something foul, obscene. Suzanne could barely stand to look at it.

We'd intended to place an ad in the paper and sell it ourselves, but our repugnance at this feculent reminder of Peter's end was too painfully intense. We made a deal with Peter's friend Mike from Catholic High to fix the minor damage and sell it himself. Mike was averse to taking any money, but Suzanne was insistent that we split the proceeds. He reluctantly agreed to these terms and took the moped to his house.

Shortly before we left for Colorado, both my sister and brother phoned, offering to fly out with us for the interment of Peter's ashes. I explained that we'd have friends and Eleanor with us, so it wasn't necessary from our point of view, but, if they felt the need themselves, they were certainly welcome. I didn't want them going to the expense and effort when it wasn't essential to us. Yet it was important to me that they understood how much their generous gesture meant to us.

CHAPTER

7

THE OPEN ROAD has always held a fascination for me, as it
does for so many. Aside from the specifics of any particular trip, I have the sense that I'm going somewhere, that
just beyond the horizon lies something new and different
and exciting; something to be found, to be seen, to be
experienced. In a sense, the quest, I suppose. As the car
pounds along the highway, I pick up a rhythm, an internal cadence, that pushes me forward. The *cla-lip, cla-
lip, cla-lip* of the tires on the pavement has a hypnotic
effect—the trance of the traveler—that urges me onward.
Just over the next ridge or across the next river is a
secret to be discovered, a mystery to be revealed. But this
trip was different.

We left for Colorado with Peter's ashes in the back of
the car. When we drive across country, we don't fool
around. We stopped the first night in Columbia, Mis-
souri, and arrived in Colorado Springs late the next afternoon. It was a dismal trip. I was constantly aware of our

cargo and the terrible contrast with earlier, happier trips out West.

I suppose there wasn't so much as a fifty-mile segment of the road west that I didn't think of Peter—or the lack of Peter. I remember a stretch between Akron and Columbus where the pain was nearly overwhelming. Suzanne was driving, so I had nothing to do but look at the lush, rolling Ohio farmland broken periodically by windbreaks of tall trees—and think of Peter. I expected to see a road sign with the legend, SLOUGH OF DESPOND. I hoped Suzanne would tire so I could drive again. The trouble with being a passenger is that you're left with nothing to do but think and reflect and feel.

I was thinking that if events had followed their normal course, I might be on this same stretch of road right now, only Peter would be driving instead of Suzanne. And, because of that *might,* I felt guilty as hell. I had planned to go to Colorado at this time anyway to see my aunt Eleanor and do some chores for her. Suzanne would not have come, as this wasn't really a vacation, but Peter had wanted to. Hence, the guilt. I hadn't wanted him along and had done my best to talk him out of the idea.

My reasons were twofold. The easy one, and the point I had made to him, was that I was going to be busy with my aunt's affairs, so he would be left with a lot of time on his hands. I would need the car a good deal of the time, which would leave him stuck at the hotel. Most of our meals would be with older people, and I was sure he would soon tire of this. I told him he would be bored and regret having come along.

The hard one, and the point I had not made to him, was that I didn't want him along. I figured he'd be a pain in the ass. Although our relationship had improved that summer, we had not been getting along very well for quite some time, so I was looking forward to being by myself. I didn't want the hassle of his asking for the car, especially at night. I didn't want the worry or the responsibility. *Where are you going? When will you be back? Be careful about this. Watch out for that. No, I don't want to go there. We haven't got time to* . . . I just didn't want to be bothered.

He had listened to my arguments, understood the points I made, but still wanted to go. At the time of his death, he still expected to go with me. For that matter, he might have. I was reluctant to say no. I had hoped he would think it over and decide against going. That would have spared my saying, in effect, "I don't like you right now, and I don't want you with me."

So he died not knowing I didn't want him with me. But I knew it, and that's what I had to deal with now. Jesus! How guilt can tear at you. It can break you down as would a ruthless interrogator, reducing you to the point where you no longer have any self-respect or self-esteem. You look into yourself and find emptiness. You're a hollow man. You get a glimpse of what Kurtz saw, and you, too, are horrified. You have reduced yourself to your lowest characteristic, and you think you've defined yourself. Pride and respect are for others, not for the likes of you. You're selfish and shallow and hypocritical. You're a pile of biological muck. Someone compliments you for a quality he detects, and you're racked with disgust. You think, *"Another one I've fooled."*

I certainly hoped I had fooled Peter, though. It was unbearable to think that he had seen through my arguments and sensed that I didn't want him with me. It was too painful even to consider that possibility. The thought was in my head, obviously, but when I tried to focus on it, to deal with it, I felt myself becoming dull. My mind simply wasn't prepared to examine the idea that he knew I was rejecting him. It was as though my brain were short-circuited, and electrical impulses caromed about erratically, throwing switches randomly and blocking any coherent pattern of thought. I couldn't find the synaptical circuit breakers to get the system functioning again. So, as we sped westward, I gave up trying to resolve the issue and told myself there was no evidence to suggest that Peter suspected the truth. I believed it. I had to.

When I said earlier, in speaking of the sympathy my group gave me in Dale's office, that I was denying the need for such consolation, I was only partially correct. In the intervening weeks I'd come to realize that I'd also been rejecting my right to sympathy because of my sense of guilt. Perhaps the most insidious element in my entire grieving process has been the feeling of guilt. It has run like an off-color thread through the fabric of my mourn-ing cloak. Guilt, real and imagined; guilt, justified and unjustified.

I didn't react well when Peter entered his teenage years and began tugging energetically at the umbilical cord that bound us together. His assertion of self and his movement toward independence was a gradual process, of course, and just as gradually, I became distant and cold. I suppose I felt threatened, even rejected. So, as I sensed his withdrawing, I withdrew myself.

One thing I have discovered about myself is that I have a terrible fear of being rejected. Between the hard times of the Depression and my mother's nervous breakdown, my parents had to send me to Colorado for close to two years to live with my aunts. I was five at the time and unable to understand why I was being sent away. Although I now realize that my parents had little choice and certainly suffered themselves, at the time I was crushed. My child's mind only understood that I was being sent away, rejected. When I was seven, I was shipped back East. This time it was my aunts who were rejecting me. For close to forty years I had repressed almost all memory of the pain and fear and anxiety attendant upon those uprootings. Only recently, for example, have I recollected what must have been one of my most distressing experiences: my father, tears in his eyes, running along the platform waving goodbye to me as the train pulled out of Grand Central. How utterly forlorn that little child must have been. I have to phrase it that way because I still can't fully recapture my feelings at the time—that child is virtually a stranger to me.

That experience, however, has been influencing my behavior all my life. In my personal relationships, especially romantic ones, at the first sign that the other person is not totally committed to me, I start to withdraw. Consequently, when Peter began his struggle with teenagehood, I was poorly prepared to help him. All I knew was that here was this ungrateful wretch pushing me away from him. My own insecurities couldn't handle it.

It's marvelous how we forget what it's like to be a teenager, to have so little control over our lives, to be ever under one authority or another, always to have to ask permission. The teenager is faced, on the one hand, by the need to be his own person and, on the other, by the need for support and guidance. He is forever trying to reconcile these conflicting tensions. I had forgotten his need to hide uncertainties and anxieties in order to appear cool. I had also forgotten—repressed, more likely —how difficult my own teens had been. I had been miserable: a rebel with a damned good cause, I had felt. The perfect hell for me would be spending eternity as a teenager.

One of the ways in which my withdrawal from Peter manifested itself was resentment. I resented his return from camp, for instance, because it meant an end to peace and quiet. After six weeks of the sublimity of Mozart and Haydn and Copland, I was again subjected to the amplified vulgarity of the Stones and the Allman Brothers. The Big Beat was back. Jethro Tull and Lynyrd Skynyrd and the Dead chased each other noisily and mindlessly through the walls of our house. I was constantly tapping on the ceiling or hollering upstairs, requesting or demanding that he turn that noise down. I was so put off by the relentless rock racket that I was unable to appreciate the importance it held for him. It divided us. I resented it and he resented my resentment.

Undoubtedly, the most significant reason for my withdrawal from Peter had nothing to do with *his* behavior or attitude. After our friend Frank died, our marriage began to fall apart. For a brief while, I thought we might separate. My self-confidence and sense of control were thoroughly shaken. Looking back, I can see that it was from this period that I began to distance myself emotionally from Peter. It was strictly a protective maneuver and an unsuccessful one at that. If Suzanne and I had split, Peter obviously would remain with her. Metaphorically, they would have put me on a train and shipped me out. The only way to deal with this contingency was not to care for him. Where's the pain in having a stranger put you on a train?

Another divisive factor in our relationship was my anger. In recent years I've come to understand that I'm a very angry person, and, significantly, that I'm terrified of my own rage. I feel like the gentle protagonist in *The Incredible Hulk* (who, in moments of rage, metamorphoses into the ferocious and destructive Hulk), when he tells another character, in a delightful piece of understatement, "You wouldn't like me when I'm angry." Consequently, I've unconsciously driven my anger underground, hidden it from myself, which has led me into countless depressions. As so often happens when I'm depressed, I retreat into myself, closing out others, especially those closest to me. As we by-passed Columbus, I convicted myself on two counts of parental malfeasance: I had shut out Peter to an extent, and I had nearly driven him from me by subjecting him to such a moody, brooding individual.

Unsurprisingly, my control was not total, and sometimes my anger would flash out unexpectedly like sun flares. One time I might ask Peter nicely, "Hey, kid, could you turn down the stereo, please?" Another day I would bellow angrily, "Shut down that goddamned noise!" I suspect he learned to move cautiously when dealing with such a volatile parent. It was a lesson he should not have learned from me.

These negative elements did not make up the whole of our relationship. They did not define it. But they were a part; a part for which I was responsible. I could not take them back; I could not undo them. I could only hope that I was being harsher on myself than Peter would have been. I didn't enjoy feeling guilty, but then again I didn't enjoy feeling cowardly either, and I couldn't respect myself if I didn't face the truth.

Fortunately, the truth is not all negative; there was much that was positive in our relationship. I wasn't feeling very positive, however, on that trip across the country.

My father's side of the family has a cemetery plot in Colorado Springs. Located on the eastern edge of town, it has many tall pines and a view of the mountains to the west. I was pleased that Suzanne wanted Peter's ashes buried there. The day after our arrival we went to a monument store across from the cemetery to order the headstone. An old man, who turned out to be the salesman, creaked out of a chair and tottered toward us. He looked as if he would be in need of his own service at any minute. We told him our purpose and chose a stone large enough for all three of us to have our names and dates inscribed on it. Suzanne and I planned to be cremated, which meant that all three of us could fit into one space in the plot. The old man shook his head sadly and said it was a bad business about Peter. We felt at ease with him.

My aunt Eleanor had us order hers as well, leaving the final date blank. The old man said it was a good idea; he had done the same thing himself.

"Isn't it disturbing to see your own tombstone?" Suzanne asked.

"Well," he smiled, "you might say it lends a kind of perspective."

To my surprise, he lit a cigarette. I said, "Don't you know that's bad for your health?" as I accepted a light myself.

He laughed and said, "None of my wife's relations smoke and they was after me for years to give it up. Most of 'em are dead now, so I reckon I'm none too worried about *their* advice."

He said the stones would be installed in one week, which gave us sufficient time to arrange with the cemetery to have the site prepared. We said goodbye to the old man and thanked him for his help.

Throughout the process of picking the headstone and style of engraving, spelling Peter's full name, and the rest of the details, I experienced another of those displacements where I seemed to stand outside myself, dispassionately observing the proceedings. "How can we be doing this?" I wondered. We appeared so calm and practical that we might have been buying silver and deciding on the style of monogram. The disparity between our purpose and our behavior was surreal. I sensed that Suzanne was imposing a rigid control upon herself. I suppose the emotional distance I felt was my way of maintaining control.

A week later, seven of us went to the cemetery for the interment (what an antiseptic word, free from any emotive contamination). Besides Eleanor, we had our friends Sam and Rusty and Dave from California, and Joe from Denver.

I had met Sam in the army. We had become friends while attending the Army Language School in Monterey and later served near each other in Korea. His wife, Rusty, and Suzanne had hit it off immediately, so we had seen a lot of each other over the years, usually when we visited them and their two children in Santa Barbara.

Sam had enjoyed Peter greatly. He used to do a lot of snorkeling and scuba diving, and he had given Peter his first lessons. They had allowed me to accompany them once, on the understanding that I'd keep out of their way and not do something silly like drowning. We had pushed out through the red tide and the kelp and had a grand time. Sam had been impressed with Peter's strength and fearlessness. He neglected to say if he had been impressed with mine.

I'd known Dave nearly as long. He lived in the town next to mine on Long Island, and we'd met just after I'd come home from the service. He was a classmate of Big Peter's in college, and, after Suzanne and Big Peter had gotten married, he'd shared a house with them for their last year of school. Shortly after Suzanne and I had married, Dave had moved to San Francisco. Nonetheless, we managed to see him fairly often. He and Peter had always been very close. One summer when Peter was ten we had rented a cabin on an old homestead in Montana near Glacier Park. Dave had visited us for a couple of weeks, and he seemed to spend more time with Peter than with us. They'd had great fun fishing and inner-tubing on the Flathead. Once we'd hiked up to a glacier, the two of them forging ahead in a race to be first. I hadn't been able to discover the winner, because they'd each claimed victory. Dave had also claimed that blisters and the thin air worked to his disadvantage—a strange complaint for a victor. I hadn't pursued the topic, however. I'd been too busy sucking wind myself.

I had met Joe through Suzanne. When he and his wife, Pat, had married, they'd rented a garage apartment from Suzanne's mother. He and Pat had a daughter a year older than Peter and a son a year younger. They'd moved to Denver before I met Suzanne, but we visited them many times on our trips West. By the time of Peter's death, Pat and Joe had been divorced for several years.

Joe had always admired Peter's self-confidence and daring. When Peter was seven, Joe took us flying in a dual-control, four-seater Cessna. He and Peter sat in front and Suzanne and I in the back. I'm still not sure what I was doing there, for I'm terrified of flying. I hold with those who believe that if God had meant man to fly, He would not have given him the interstate highway system. That flight did nothing to change my mind. Every time we hit turbulence or air pockets, I hit a new high in terror. Then Joe asked Peter if he would like to fly the plane a while.

"Pull back on the stick a bit," he told Peter. Peter obeyed and the nose rose slowly, taking us higher and higher above the solid, firm, lovely ground where we belonged.

Joe said, "That's good. Now ease the control forward to where it was." We were flying level now, the Air Force Academy a mere speck below us. I was about to shout for oxygen when I realized I was holding my breath. Joe was half turned in his seat, one hand near his control column, telling Suzanne what a marvelous plane it was—how all kinds of things could go wrong, yet he could still land it safely.

"You're doing great, Peter," Joe said to him, his eyes scanning the sky for other aircraft. "Push the stick forward a little and see what happens."

Peter pushed it quite a little and several things happened: we dive-bombed the Academy chapel, and my stomach landed in my throat. The ground was racing up to us with alarming rapidity when Joe laughed and took control again. "That was a little more than I meant, Peter," he said easily. The Red Baron nodded, satisfied that he had taken out the chapel on his first attempt.

Such remembrances were flitting through my mind as I looked at our little group standing around the small grave site. I knew it was a sacrifice on Sam and Rusty's part, as well as Dave's, to fly to Colorado on short notice. Aside from the expense of the trip, Sam and Dave were using vacation days that they had planned to put to happier use. That made their presence all the more important to us.

I got the cardboard-wrapped urn from our car and brought it over. Joe offered to take it from me, but I felt it was something I had to do myself. As I placed it in the prepared hole, I was surprised to see that there was a cement form embedded in the ground. I fitted a cover over the form and picked up the small shovel, not much larger than an entrenching tool, that I had bought earlier. I gently shoveled in a couple of loads of dirt and handed the shovel to Suzanne. She did the same and passed it on until everyone had helped fill the hole. We then placed a piece of sod on top. We all stood silently for a few minutes, those who were so inclined, no doubt, praying.

Suzanne had wanted to say a communal prayer, but she started crying and couldn't speak. She had felt a steel-banded constriction around her chest from the moment we got to our plot and saw the small, square hole in the ground. She knew that Peter was no more, his spirit or essence no longer here, so why was putting his ashes in the ground so crushingly painful? She felt that Peter was present in our thoughts and could well be enjoying a spiritual life. Why then, she wondered, did this symbolic physical place trigger such a gut-rending response?

The one consolation she experienced was the absolute conviction that we were right in having Peter cremated. She felt she could not have borne the thought that his *body* was in the ground, engulfed in the loneliness and silence, the coldness and wetness, subject to the ignominy of corporeal disintegration. She suspected that as time went by she would have speculated about the stage of decay his body was in, what inroads the course of nature had made, what obscenities had been committed upon the flesh of her flesh. To have left his body in that far place would have been nearly impossible, but leaving his ashes, while difficult, was bearable. Just. Reduced to ashes, Peter had ceased to be as Suzanne had known him.

Standing at that grave site, I again experienced one of those moments when the full impact of Peter's death consumed my entire being. I knew I'd been dealt a terrible blow. Something had happened that I was powerless to do anything about. I had no recourse, and no illusions that I had even the slightest control in determining the outcome. I couldn't talk my way out of this one. No compromises, no options, no alternative. Just the single, terrible, irrevocable fact of his death. That absolute, eternal fact. My sense of impotence was so overwhelming that I felt like one of Thackeray's puppets, only my strings were being controlled by a malignant puppeteer.

As I stood holding Suzanne's hand, I looked closely for the first time at that god-awful headstone. In my worst fantasies about Peter, I had never pictured so explicitly the consequences of his death. I had never imagined his nightmare marker. I had never seen his name carved in stone. I had never seen those pathetically few years inscribed in granite.

The place and the mood called to mind an incident that happened a couple of years before. Peter and I had been having a fight about some reckless behavior of his, and I had told him that someday he could dance on my grave, but for now he was going to do as I said. My judgment would have to prevail until he developed more common sense. Now, I thought, he'll not be able to dance on my grave. For a hysterical moment I saw myself jumping up and down on his grave in a grotesque parody of a dance, screaming, *"I told you. I warned you. Why didn't you listen?"*

The lines of a Cummings poem that I'd often used with my students, on the fragility of life, ran through my mind:

> plato told
>
> him:he couldn't
> believe it(jesus

```
told him;he
wouldn't believe
it)lao

tsze
certainly told
him,and general
(yes

mam)
sherman;
and even
(believe it
or

not)you
told him:i told
him;we told him
(he didn't believe it,no

sir)it took
a nipponized bit of
the old sixth

avenue
el;in the top of his head:to tell

him
```

"*A nice paradox,*" I thought: "*that woke him up, dead.*"
I felt empty, devoid of substance, as though I'd been
eviscerated. I looked again at the grave. How long, I
wondered, before the wood rotted, the cement crumbled,

the metal disintegrated, and the ashes became part of the earth? I'm neither religious nor superstitious, so I attached no supernatural significance to the proceedings or to the site, yet I couldn't shake the feeling that Peter was watching or at least aware of us. For the first time I understood the compulsion of people who try to make contact with those who have "passed over." I also realized that I was probably engaging in a form of denial, refusing to accept the absolute finality of death. But what the hell did that matter? Peter was dead and buried and I felt as though part of me were buried there as well.

A couple of days later Suzanne and I took Dave to see a few of the old mining towns back in the mountains. As we were walking around Cripple Creek, I fell into a foul mood. I became sullen and remote. These moods were nothing new with me, but since Peter's death I'd made a prodigious effort to keep them under control. I knew my behavior was disturbing Suzanne, but I couldn't shake my bad humor.

That night when we were alone, she gave me hell. "I'm not going to take any more of this crap from you. If you're going to act that way, you can take a hike. I mean it. I was so upset coming down Ute Pass that I was crying —because my ally wasn't here. If Peter were here, he'd have given me a look that said, 'There he goes again,' and everything would have been all right. I realized then that he and I had been allies, at least when you were being a bastard. Together we could put up with your brooding bad temper. But now I don't have him for support, and I'm not going to put up with your nonsense alone. You'd better understand that!"

She was right, of course, and I felt rotten. I apologized and promised to work really hard at improving. This was the first time we'd had words since Peter's death; the first schism in our united front against the common enemy, grief. It would not be the last one.

CHAPTER

8

WE RETURNED HOME at the end of August. We were both extremely depressed, and it took us a while before we realized the reason. We were stunned by the sense of returning to an empty house. We were accustomed to having Peter away at camp during the summer months, but he was always home by this time of year. Our shock was all the more profound because we were completely unprepared for it. We had not anticipated the problem of finding the house empty. For the first time, Peter's absence, as distinguished from his death, made itself felt.

Suzanne went back to work a couple of days later and reexperienced the distress of her earlier return. A number of people had been on vacation at the time of Peter's death, so Suzanne had to go through it all again with them. She did, however, find it easier this time. Gradually, she resumed her routine, and before long she discovered to her surprise that she preferred working to being around the house. At home she had more free time, time to think and feel, time to brood and hurt.

But, of course, there was really no escaping the pain. Since we both work, Suzanne and I had divided the domestic chores for years. One of my jobs was the grocery shopping. I would buy Peter a six-pack of soda and a bag of snacks when I did the weekly shopping. Any goodies beyond those, excepting desserts, he had to buy himself. As I always shopped at the same store, I had a set routine and automatically picked up those items we normally used. The first time I shopped after Peter's death I found myself reaching for some root beer, when I realized there was no need for it any more. I stood there, staring stupidly at the root beer, completely nonplussed. As pain began to well up, I reflected that shopping would be less expensive from now on. But that happy thought didn't make the pain go away. To hell with cynicism—it wasn't working anyway. I got out of that aisle in a hurry, hoping I could leave the pain with the root beer.

One of the first things I did was to search again for that blasted safe-deposit key. It seemed so easy when Marlowe or Archer looked for something, but I had no luck. When Peter's friend Mark stopped by one day, he volunteered to try his hand. In less than twenty minutes he handed me the key: It had been taped to the wall behind one of Peter's rock posters. Who wants to be a detective anyway?

We canceled the locksmith and went to the bank. We already had authorization to open the box for inventory purposes, and, with a bank vice president hovering over us, that's what we did. We were both feeling slightly sick with apprehension as Suzanne lifted the top. What an agreeable anticlimax: it was empty. I had been quietly nursing a righteous anger at Peter, anticipating the unpleasantness we would suffer at finding a stash of grass or pills or God-knows-what. I felt the anger drain away, replaced by a mixture of relief and guilt. Once again, I had expected the worst where Peter was concerned. Suzanne caught my eye, her face triumphant at the acquittal of our son from our mutual indictment. I winked my agreement.

One of Peter's best friends stopped by. Ricky and Peter had met at King in the sixth grade and had been fast friends ever since. They had gone to a couple of summer camps together, the last one a sailing camp in the Virgin Islands where Peter had gotten his scuba certification. Ricky was on a bus tour of the West when Peter was killed. His parents had decided not to interrupt, much less ruin, his vacation by notifying him at the time. Upon his return they told him, and he was furious.

Ricky and I were friends as well. He'd been a student of mine for years and currently was one of my seniors. I explained to him that it's a risky business making decisions for other people, that his parents had been faced with a dilemma. If our positions were reversed, I told him, we probably would have made the same decision. We had a long talk, Suzanne and I going over the old ground again. It became neither easier nor harder with each retelling, although it hurt each time to see the pain our account was causing. Suzanne gave Ricky a three-piece pin-striped suit that Big Peter had given Peter for his last birthday. As Peter had loved the suit, it warmed us to see that Ricky was genuinely pleased with it.

Ricky told us about an incident that had occurred

shortly after Peter started attending King. A group of kids were playing Frisbee during recess. As the new boy, Peter was receiving a lot of guff, especially from Ricky. It soon got out of hand, and the two of them began fighting. Peter knocked Ricky to the ground and began pummeling the devil out of him. Peter then asked Ricky if he'd give up. Ricky wouldn't, so Peter hit him again. This was repeated several times before Peter let him up. "That began our friendship," Ricky said. "I respected Peter because he was stronger, and I could tell he wasn't really trying to hurt me. He respected me because I was too pig-headed to give up."

I would soon be seeing Ricky at school, but I felt as sad as Suzanne did when he left. It was as though a link to Peter had been broken.

School was to reopen on September 11. I had a great deal of preparing to do, and it seemed to take forever. Organization, at which I had considered myself good, escaped me. I seemed to spend a lot of time at my desk accomplishing very little. Concentration was beyond me. It wasn't that I was consciously thinking of Peter, although that happened too, but I just couldn't seem to focus my attention on the business at hand. It didn't worry me at the time, for I figured once I got back into the routine of the school year my old habits of work would reappear. I was wrong.

Suzanne's birthday fell on September 10th. I say *fell* because it landed between us with a dull thud. Although birthdays don't mean much to me, they meant a great deal to Suzanne, as they had to Peter. We'd always gone out to dinner, the birthday person choosing the restaurant. Once, on Suzanne's birthday, we had gone to a restaurant in Greenwich where the waiters like to surround the table of a birthday celebrant and bellow the Happy Birthday song at the top of their lungs. Suzanne despises public displays where she's concerned, and Peter and I had nearly driven her wild pretending to signal the waiter that it was her birthday. It was pure bluff, though; even Peter was not reckless enough to provoke his mother in that way.

Before we would go out to dinner, the presents would be opened. For the past several years, Peter had given his mother cheese. This year, we had decided to go ahead and celebrate Suzanne's birthday. I was rushing about looking for presents when I passed a cheese shop. Without hesitating, I bought her a couple of cheeses, both of which Peter had given her in the past. The curious point is that I didn't do it intentionally. I intended no gesture.

As Suzanne was opening her presents, it dawned on me what I had done: I had never in my life given her cheese. When she saw the cheese, she was nearly overcome. I started to explain that I had acted unconsciously, but she cut me off. She was very pleased with the cheese and said, however it had happened, she was happy to have gotten it. She felt this was a sign. Peter was giving her the cheese and was using me as his vehicle to make his presence known. We both had tears in our eyes. It was a bittersweet moment.

We had planned to dine out, and I had arranged with Jane and Michael for them to meet us at the restaurant. Suzanne hates surprises, but I knew she wouldn't mind with good friends like Jane and Michael. She didn't, but it was a difficult evening for her. Peter's absence was more pronounced than his presence had sometimes been. Both Suzanne and Michael got loaded, Suzanne jabbering away like a magpie throughout dinner. Later, when Suzanne and I talked about the evening, we agreed that on its own terms it had been fun. Only when compared to what it might have been did it fall short.

When school began, I was startled at how difficult it was. To begin with, I was extremely uncomfortable. I was tense, and I sensed a tension in many of the students. Superficially, they were as friendly and warm as usual, but I felt a reserve, almost a shyness, on the part of many of them. There was less teasing and wisecracking than usual, and no one asked how my summer had been, a common question in the past. I felt this circumstance to be especially pronounced with the seniors.

One of the hats I wore was that of senior adviser, so the seniors were an official responsibility of mine. This class would have been Peter's had he remained at King, and I had known most of the boys for years, so I felt a personal responsibility as well. We had a little time before a general assembly, so I asked the seniors to gather in my homeroom. After dispensing with some routine matters, I spoke to them about Peter and about myself.

I told them how low I was feeling and that I knew some of them were down also. I said that my wife and I were facing Peter's death as directly and openly as we could, and those of them who were friends of Peter's would be well advised to do the same. I said I didn't want Peter's death to come between us, for it to pose a barrier they were reluctant to cross. They should feel free to speak to me at any time about anything that was bothering them, including Peter. They shouldn't hesitate to bring up his name for fear of hurting me, because the pain and hurt were there anyway. Insofar as our relationship went, I told them, they should continue to be the miserable, wretched creatures they had always been. If they suddenly turned into little angels, I would feel uncomfortable and be highly suspicious. I said that despite what had happened I was still interested in them, wanted them to have as good a senior year as possible and to get into the best colleges that they were able to. I stressed that if they sensed I was behaving differently or seemed depressed, they shouldn't avoid speaking to me about it. I reiterated a point I often made with my students that nothing is so bad that talking about it makes it worse.

The bell rang, signaling that the entire school should assemble in the study hall. While Gardiner was welcoming everyone back, I looked out over the sea of bright, shining faces and felt a surge of rage flow through me. I saw myself lobbing a hand grenade into the center of that sea. I wanted to blast those faces into that same oblivion that had claimed Peter. Why were they here and he not? Why had this happened to him? Why had this happened to me? Surely there were more worthy candidates for suffering than I.

When my rage began to ebb, I marveled at the depth of my feeling. Did I really want to kill them? Did I hate them that much for being alive? This would be a sweet school year if I really felt that way. I was too upset to make much sense of it. I tried to concentrate on what Gardiner was saying. It didn't hold my attention, so I slipped out and went over to my office in the library. I sat at my desk and looked at all the books and reports and papers—and wondered what I was doing there. I had never doubted my teaching ability in the past, but teaching takes a lot of energy and enthusiasm, and I didn't feel I had much of either now. What did I care if people wanted to sometimes split infinitives or use prepositions to end sentences with? Dangle your participles, my boys; what does it ultimately matter? We're all dangling, in a manner of speaking.

To my surprise, I fell quickly into the old routine and was soon boring the boys with all my accustomed verve and style. My greatest problem remained my lack of concentration. I had always prided myself on getting work back speedily to my students. In fact, I often had students express surprise, if not chagrin, at the suddenness with which retribution fell upon their efforts. I emphasized to new teachers the importance of returning written work quickly. I was really astonished, then, to discover that even the most routine and familiar assignments were taking me nearly twice as long to finish.

This led to frustration because I felt a self-imposed pressure to maintain my normal timetable. I soon realized, however, that I couldn't keep both my schedule and my sanity. I moved to a less ambitious schedule but felt that I was indulging myself. I decided this was to be a temporary expedient.

When I corrected student papers, my habit was to read the essay through, getting a general sense of the writer's intention and the quality of his execution of that intention. I would then go through the paper sentence by sentence, making corrections and suggestions as well as complimenting that which was done well. But I was now horrified to find that on first reading, and even second and third, I couldn't fathom the writer's purpose or decipher what was wrong with his paper. I couldn't determine if it was a brilliantly reasoned argument or utter drivel. I felt like a novice teacher who doesn't know where to begin. It seemed as though each paper belonged to that frustrating category that are so abysmally written that they virtually defy correction. I found myself getting up earlier and working later in order to meet even my new, less exacting schedule.

The problem of concentration is a fascinating one. As I noted earlier, it wasn't a question of my actively thinking of Peter, or daydreaming in the conventional sense. I simply couldn't focus for any length of time on the matter at hand. This wasn't only a problem in correcting papers, I found, for I also had difficulty listening to others speak. A student would be making a point that I had completely lost track of, and I would be forced to fall back on the old pedagogical ploy of saying, "That's certainly an interesting point. I wonder if anyone has a comment on it?" I would then search the faces of the brighter or more talkative students, desperately looking for a response.

I found that my lack of concentration was not restricted to work but fell over into the social sphere as well. Even interesting conversations or discussions would fail to keep my attention. Again, I wouldn't be thinking about anything specific; my mind just seemed to close down. I felt I should wear a sign: SORRY, MIND TEMPORARILY OUT OF ORDER. I supposed I was using so much psychic energy grieving that I was mentally worn out. Psychological exhaustion of some sort.

For the most part, however, my teaching didn't suffer,

and the classroom experience was much as it always had been. I found that I was responding to the students as I had in the past, and the early feeling of resentment gradually faded. Occasionally, though, something would occur which would upset me terribly, break my rhythm, and reduce me to near incoherence. An instance of this happened in my eleventh-grade section when we were studying *Macbeth*.

We were examining that section of the play in which Macduff has gone to England to join forces with Malcolm, the rightful heir. Unbeknownst to Macduff, Macbeth has had his wife and children murdered. Malcolm, fearing Macduff may be an agent of Macbeth's, tests him by pretending he possesses the characteristics of a tyrant. Macduff refuses to serve him until Malcolm reveals that he does, in fact, have the requisite princely virtues. Shakespeare thus introduces the unorthodox notion, for his time, of a subject passing judgment on his sovereign, a point I stress to my students.

I had read and taught *Macbeth* so often that for the past couple of years I had not reread it. I had forgotten that immediately after Macduff and Malcolm are reconciled, word is brought that Macduff's family has been slaughtered. I was floored by the impact of Macduff's receiving this devastating news. In disbelief he says, "My children too?" Those words leaped off the page at me. My mind blanked and I had the old difficulty breathing. I completely lost track of the point I was making. I wasn't concerned that the kids knew I was shaken; I was too entangled in my own feelings. I was reexperiencing the sensations I had felt that Wednesday morning a few months before. The complete unexpectedness of the attack made it all the more unsettling. Luckily, this incident happened toward the end of the class, so the disruption was minimal. For a brief moment I had felt self-conscious and foolish, reverting to the old nonsense that it wasn't manly to let others know you were grieving—but that quickly passed. However, I did feel an overwhelming need to be alone. As I was free for the next hour. I drove to a nearby diner and sat in a booth drinking coffee, wondering if it would be like this forever.

CHAPTER

9

IN SEPTEMBER, we attended our first Compassionate Friends meeting. The Compassionate Friends, to quote its national newsletter, "is a self-help organization offering friendship and understanding to bereaved parents. The purposes are to promote and aid parents in the positive resolution of the grief experienced upon the death of their child, and to foster the physical and emotional health of bereaved parents and siblings." The Compassionate Friends is a national organization with chapters in most states. Each chapter has a chairperson, and most chapters issue their own newsletters. Our chapter meets once a month, although some meet biweekly.

We have found Compassionate Friends to be immensely helpful, and we know others for whom it has made all the difference. Without Compassionate Friends, they either would not have come to terms with their grief, or they would have taken much longer to do so.

When first informed about Compassionate Friends, Suzanne and I were sympathetic to the idea, in large part because of our group experience with Dale. We had learned the benefits that accrue from an open, direct, and honest expression of feelings; consequently, we felt none of the aversion to such an encounter that we subsequently discovered many others do. Also, although I thought I was handling my grief well, 'I did have some doubts. I didn't know whether or not certain of my responses to Peter's death were abnormal. I wanted reassurance that my feelings of rage and guilt and helplessness were typical. I wanted confirmation that my suicidal feelings, as opposed to intentions, were characteristic. I wanted to be sure that I wasn't losing my mind and just kidding myself that I was coping adequately.

At that first meeting there were about twenty people present. Although there were several couples, the women outnumbered the men by nearly three to one. This, we discovered, is fairly common; men are more resistant to talking about their grief. Pat, our chairwoman, after dealing with some old business, made a blunt, direct comment that got to the essence of our situation, "Don't try to deny the injury that has been done you; don't try to deny that you are hurt. You've lost a child and that's why you're here." She then had each of us introduce ourselves and give a brief account of our child's death. No one had to speak, nor was there any pressure to do so. Suzanne and I were among the most recently bereaved; others had been so for anywhere from one to five years.

One of the most beneficial aspects of Compassionate

Friends for us was listening to those who were further down the road. To my mind, one bereaved parent's advice is worth that of a dozen professionals'. Without meaning to strike an anti-intellectual note, I think that there are certain areas of human experience that are not particularly accessible through the theoretical approach. I've looked through a good amount of the literature on death, and much of it is useless and some of it downright harmful. In all fairness, I must admit this to be a purely subjective reaction. Our chapter has a fairly extensive book and tape library which is constantly being used. Most of the bereaved parents we know read widely in the genre. I read one book in which the author rattled on at great length about the "stages of grief." It was a splendid argument, well reasoned and persuasive. The only problem is that I've yet to meet a bereaved parent who underwent any such progression of steps. The book created false expectations.

In many ways, Compassionate Friends reminds me of Alcoholics Anonymous. Both are self-help groups, both contain support systems, and both tolerate professionals by invitation only. Most important, however, both are the most effective vehicles I know of for helping their respective members to reorder their lives.

Perhaps the most salutary information I gleaned from that first meeting concerned the problem of concentration. I discovered that I had a lot of company. It was particularly helpful to hear a couple of high-powered New York executives say that they experienced, and to an extent were still experiencing, difficulties similar to those I was undergoing. They told me not to worry about it, that my concentration would gradually return, and, until it did, there was little I could do about it. "What you must understand," one of them said, "is that you're in a different ball game now. The officials have changed the rules on you in the middle of the game, and you need time to readjust. Don't try to rush it." The other chap pointed out something I was in the process of discovering myself: learn your new limitations and work within them.

Listening to the others talk, Suzanne and I benefited from realizing that individuals grieve differently. This had caused several couples additional problems. The women, it appeared, tended to be more open and demonstrative in expressing their grief. The effect of their children's deaths seemed to have greater impact upon their everyday lives. Obversely, the men seemed to adjust sooner or, at least, express their grief less openly. I have heard that the incidence of hypertension, migraine headaches, ulcers, and even coronary disorders is more prevalent among bereaved fathers than mothers. If this is true, it suggests that men tend to repress their grief more. Whatever the case, grief is stressful, and, if poorly handled, can lead to serious complications.

Based on my own unscientific observations, I would agree that men deal fairly poorly with grief. Too often, they seem to have bought the macho fallacy that silence and stoicism are virile qualities and that acknowledging grief is a sign of weakness. I suspect, too, that men are more threatened than women by the loss of a child. Nothing brings home to you more forcibly your powerlessness and lack of control than the death of your child. Since men are generally presumed to have more power and exert greater control in our society ("Let Dad do it; he can handle it"), their self-confidence is at greater risk. Add to that the myth of male self-sufficiency and you have a guy with problems, especially if he thinks, *"Would Gary Cooper or John Wayne join some group to talk about how much they're hurting, to look for help? Hell, no. They'd just suck in their gut and do what a man has to do."* It's seldom explained, however, what it is a man has to do—short of shooting up the prairie. Could it be that they're so fast with their guns because they're so slow with their mouths?

Sadly, in real life, there is little for a man to do except to lose himself in his work or in some other escape such as alcohol. Unless, that is, he squarely faces the fact that his only recourse is to acknowledge that he is hurting, that his power is severely limited, that he has little control over his environment, and that he needs help and support. Then he might find out who and what he really is, and, curiously enough, it might not be so bad. He might realize there's a lot more to life than riding off into the sunset, sitting tall in the saddle.

To put it another way, I think a paramount reason for many of us men being resistant to the idea of Compassionate Friends, or of seeking outside help, is that we would have to admit publicly, as well as to ourselves, that we don't have the answer, or answers, to those unanswerable questions bereaved parents ask. Our competence is limited. Here's a problem we can't solve. Mr. Fixit is stymied. We are forced to face our helplessness. That kind of self-knowledge is painful to acquire; it is also a collateral consequence of losing your child.

"What did you think of the meeting?" Suzanne asked on the way home.

"I thought it was really helpful," I said. "I'm glad we went."

"So am I, but it was depressing. God, was it depressing. Those stories and all the loose ends."

Indeed, we had heard some real horror stories. One couple's child had drowned that July at a summer camp in Canada. Ahead of them yet was a return to Canada for the inquest. They said there might have been negligence, and they were distraught at the ugliness that implied. Should they retain counsel? Did they have an obligation to pursue the matter legally in order to protect other children? Loose ends . . . that protract the pain.

Several couples had lost their children through suicide. In one case it was uncertain that it was suicide, which added a nasty twist to their grief. It became clear to us that the parents of suicides experienced feelings of responsibility and guilt and self-accusation far beyond those that the rest of us felt. They had to live with the fact that their children found life so unbearable and were undergoing such utter despair that suicide seemed the only alternative for them. Loose ends . . . that prevent the healing.

The teenage daughter of another couple was raped and murdered. They had to contend not only with her death but also with the nature of her dying. Their imaginations gave them no respite from the ghastly images of her final hour or two, and the terror and agony the girl must have experienced. They had to live with the search for the killer, and then his apprehension, insanity plea, trial, verdict, and sentencing—all of which could stretch over years. Loose ends . . . that unravel in the night.

My conviction that Compassionate Friends was a valuable outfit was not formed after just one meeting, but after several. By then I had come to realize a number of points about Compassionate Friends and other bereaved parents. I had a feeling of ease and unconstraint with them that I seldom had with others. I never felt I was making them uncomfortable simply by being present. I never had to watch what I said for fear of reminding them of the dark side of life. I never had to put on a front with them.

I noticed that we had started dividing people into two groups: us and them. Those that knew what it was like to lose a child and those who could only imagine what it was like. Admittedly, we didn't feel that with most of our closest friends, whose emphathy bridged the gap between us. But in a general sense we felt it, as did virtually all of the bereaved parents we came to know. We developed a siege mentality to an extent.

At every meeting we heard tales of the pain caused by the insensitivity of *them*. Perhaps the most devastating question a bereaved parent can be asked is, "Are you over it yet?" What makes the question so deadly is the implication that you should be. Unless there's a psychological problem, one recovers from—gets over, as it were—other deaths. Although many people recognize that there's a profound difference in a child's death, they don't grasp the full significance of it for the parents. So you get asked and you're stung.

For people who don't have the advantage of Compassionate Friends (or at least some sort of crisis counseling), who, in that sense, are isolated in their grief, such a question can cause added complications. They begin to wonder what's wrong with them. Why haven't they snapped out of it yet? Why are they still wallowing in their misery? I know several people who came to Compassionate Friends late in their grieving process whose recovery had been hindered by that insidious question.

I realize, certainly, that people don't always mean the question as crudely as it sounds. They may really be asking, "Are you past the shock stage?" or, "Are you able to function again?" But it doesn't sound that way to a bereaved parent.

A couple of times friends or good acquaintances, who have seldom or never spoken to us about Peter, have told us, while under the influence of a good many drinks, how shaken they were by his death and how sorry they are for us. It's an awkward moment. We accept their gestures in the spirit in which they're given, but their lubricated sincerity makes us uncomfortable. We see good, decent people who are perplexed by a grief they don't understand. This has formed a barrier between us.

"I don't understand how you can wallow in your misery," is one of the favorite statements made by husbands who object to their wives joining Compassionate Friends. Or, they may not oppose their wives attending, but they have no intention of "wallowing" themselves. This attitude, of course, represents a complete misunderstanding of the function of Compassionate Friends. Compassionate Friends encourages you to *deal* with your grief, not *wallow* in it. The whole thrust of Compassionate

Friends is to help you adjust to your new situation, not surrender to it.

Far from being "wallowers," we want to shed our grief. We want to get as quickly as we can to that point where the pain of living no longer outweighs the pleasure of living. We won't want to forget or repress; we want to adjust. Although there are pain and tears at our meetings, there are also warmth and laughter. We hurt, but we work at being healed.

This is not to say that I found every minute of our meetings rewarding. Sometimes, in the earlier sessions, I found myself playing Who-Hurts-More. I started from the premise that no one hurt as much as we did. I'd look at a couple who lost a baby, and I'd think, *"We hurt more. We had seventeen years of knowing Peter. He was an individualized entity with his own character and personality. Babies are little more than noisy cabbages, barely differentiated from one another. Clearly, we hurt more."* Someone else lost a nineteen-year-old in an accident. The youngster lived a week, and the parents watched him slowly die. *"They must hurt more. But wait a minute— Peter was an only child, but they have two other kids. We probably hurt more."* The child of another couple committed suicide. *"That had to be about the worst."* I was sure they hurt more than we.

Even as I was indulging myself in this contest of comparative pain, I realized I was being asinine. It was a foolish and unrewarding pastime, but I couldn't avoid engaging in it. I realized, of course, that there was no good age for one's child to die; any age is the worst for that parent. Nor does it matter if it was an only child; the pain is just as severe, even if there are several surviving children. This contest didn't last for long, but it was bothersome. Eventually, I mentioned my game to a couple of bereaved friends. They were familiar with it. I was glad to hear I wasn't the only player.

Although there wasn't much discussion of sex at our meetings, we soon found from private conversations that we'd been no different from many bereaved couples, in that sex was a problem at first. We both had been dreading it. I was aware of several inhibiting factors.

The most obvious was that since the sexual act is to a large extent psychological, a fantasy playland of sorts, it's difficult to generate exciting fantasies when your psyche is consumed with grief. The interest just isn't there. Furthermore, how could you allow yourself the pleasure of this marvelous experience when your child is dead? With Peter dead, we had no right to happiness, to enjoy ourselves. Sex seemed inappropriate. Lastly, sex is, after all, the act of procreation, the act which brought Peter into being, so he and his death were inseparable from the act in our minds. This consideration was more effective than a cold shower in dampening my rutting instincts.

When it finally happened with us, probably in the third week, it was unplanned and uneventful. In a way, we were seeking comfort and reassurance more than pleasure. More important, we'd cleared a hurdle that had threatened to complicate our already difficult lives.

Often in our meetings, people brought up the subject of God. As I don't believe in such a being, these discussions were irrelevant to me. But they did occasion some reflections on my part.

One of the most striking complaints that I've heard

from many, but certainly not all, bereaved parents concerns the poor quality of help they received from their spiritual advisers, be they Protestant, Catholic, or Jewish. Far too often the advice offered by these spokesmen of God, many of whom were unmarried and childless themselves, was sentimental and platitudinous. Several couples I know were informed that "Your child was only loaned to you." What in the world does a bereaved parent do with that? It sounds as though the child were repossessed by the Heavenly Finance Corporation because the parents had fallen into celestial arrears.

Another appalling spiritual banality delivered to two couples was that "God needed little —————— more than you did." Of all the syrupy tripe to foist on someone suffering the agony of having lost a child, this one, to my mind, stands unsurpassed. The insensitivity and arrogance implicit in the remark are mind-boggling. It would be amusing if it weren't so brutal. One couple was so outraged that they haven't been to church since. In the other case, because of this and other comments, the mother was made to feel that divine retribution had befallen her. She assumed moral responsibility for her child's death, which in turn lengthened and made more difficult her grieving process.

Often, parents were told to pray, to put their trust in God, and not to lose their faith. Several parents have told me they got the impression that their minister-priest-rabbi was more concerned with keeping them in the flock than with ministering to their sorrow. Others, of course, found solace and strength in turning to prayer, in trusting God. If that helps them, terrific. But far too often the advice tends to be otherworldly; hence too abstract and remote to be of much use in dealing with the immediate emotional crisis the bereaved are undergoing.

Along this line is the suggestion that parents should "think of the day when you and your loved one, indeed, all your loved ones, will be reunited in the presence of God." To the religious-minded this happy thought must be comforting. To hold the conviction that you will again be with your child, or any loved one—I've always wondered if that included pets—must be of immeasurable comfort. The idea makes me wish I could believe. I'm sure it would take the edge off my sorrow.

Some fall away from organized religion and others turn to it. And some religious people undergo a shattering experience when they realize that they're enraged with God for taking their children, or allowing their children to be taken. One mother had been nearly crushed at feeling such emotions. Luckily, she had a wise priest who told her that a God who could do and be all the things we attribute to Him could certainly handle her anger. "Get it out of your system," he said. "God will understand." We need more like him. As with other types of professionals, the clergy is not well prepared to deal with death or the grieving process. Turning to them is as chancy as turning to any shingle-hanger. You may get a good person or you may get a dud. With Compassionate Friends, however, you're not going to an individual but to a group; consequently, one person's bad advice is countered by several people's good advice.

Some of the most helpful counsel we received from Compassionate Friends concerned anticipating difficult and unpleasant situations. We were warned, for example, that holidays would be a problem. Aside from the pain a normally happy occasion like Christmas would bring, we were told to be prepared for cards from distant, uninformed friends with whom we corresponded only at that time. They'd probably include your child in the greeting, perhaps ask questions about what he was doing, and tell you what their kids were up to. At any time, your child might receive a letter from an old friend, perhaps a pal he'd met at camp; or receive a magazine renewal, or an invitation, or. . . .

In late October there was a phone call for Peter. A job he had once applied for was now available. Was he still interested? Even though I had been forewarned of such an eventuality, I found the call upsetting. It activated my grieving mechanism, bringing to the surface again my terrible sense of loss and my overwhelming sense of unfairness. I was awash in self-pity. I felt like a child who screams, "It's not fair!" How many times as a child had I or one of my companions cried out "Not fair" as some injustice, real or imagined, was inflicted upon us? I suppose we never entirely lose that part of ourselves.

That phone call did momentarily catch me off guard. For an instant I stopped to think about where he was— at school? in his room?—before memory responded with the hateful answer. Repeatedly, in the first few months I kept *forgetting* that Peter was dead. That is, I would be going about my business, when the fact that he was dead would enter my consciousness. Or more often, I would see or hear something and think, *"Peter will be interested in that,"* and immediately, usually with a jolt, I would remember that he was dead.

Another way in which Compassionate Friends was helpful to us, although painful as well, was the opportunity it provided for listening to stories of parents whose children had been murdered, died by suicide, or died as a result of possible negligence. These accounts made us realize how relatively fortunate we were. Peter's death had been clean and fast. We had to deal only with his death, while these other parents had to deal with the manner of their children's dying. Many friends had told us to take comfort that Peter had not suffered. Believe me, we did. But what does one say to these other parents?

Suzanne and I have noticed that in the accidental death of a young child, the destructive element of blame enters. One parent blames the other for not properly supervising the little one. The accusatory questions begin to fly: What were you doing when she drowned or fell out of the tree? How long was he out of your sight? Sadly, in their time of greatest need for each other, these parents are driven apart, alienated from one another. Even more terrible, of course, are the self-accusations with which these bereaved parents condemn themselves.

It's easy for a bereaved parent to blame himself. In the early months I certainly did. If we hadn't moved to Connecticut; if only I'd woken sooner, if . . . sure—and if wishes were horses then beggars would ride, as my mother-in-law likes to say.

I've spoken to several bereaved parents about this phenomenon, and it seems to me that in our unwillingness to accept the idea that life is a random, inexplicable, and unordered affair, we are prepared to blame ourselves. We are too threatened by the concept of an absurd, chaotic existence. If no other reason presents itself, we are liable to reproach ourselves rather than admit this unpalatable fact. To say you're responsible is to imply that you have control, and we all like, if not need, to think we possess this quality. In a way, it's safer for the self to say, "I'm at fault," than to say, "I'm helpless."

Peter's death certainly made me feel helpless. It reinforced my sense of the absurdity of life as had no other death in my experience. Since death is the next logical step to old age, the death of a parent or grandparent, for example, doesn't disturb our conviction of an ordered universe.

The history of man, in one sense, is the attempt to impose order and meaning upon a seemingly chaotic and irrational world. All the great thinkers, be they philosophers, scientists, or poets, have sought to give shape and sense to the random elements of existence. Each of us, often in a less conscious and less disciplined way, tries to impose order on and give meaning to his life. Peter's death shook the foundation of the fragile structure we had erected, and the whole edifice came tumbling down. For us, the earth was again without form, and void; and darkness was upon the face of the deep. Purpose and meaning were shattered—only blind, instinctive survival remained.

Related to recognizing my helplessness was realizing that I was a victim. It's not hard to accept abstractly that most of us are victims at one point or another, but to accept that at *this* time and in *this* circumstance I am unequivocally a victim, is not an uplifting experience. It's destructive to your sense of well-being. It's reductive, in that you feel you are less than you had assumed you were. You feel yourself a failure.

I was very conscious of feeling that I had failed as a parent because my child was dead. Parents are supposed to see to it that their children grow to adulthood. This is not so much proclaimed as it is assumed; nonetheless, it is there. That "still, small voice" tells you that you have not measured up. In your joust with life, you have been unhorsed and everyone knows it. You cannot remount because in this tournament there are no second chances, and you feel the eyes of the crowd upon you as you leave the field in disgrace.

CHAPTER

10

IN THE FALL, the school trustees held a cocktail party for
the faculty at the headmaster's house. It was a pleasant
way for them to meet new faculty and for new members of
the board to meet those of us they didn't already know.
With wives, or in some cases husbands, along, it was a
large assemblage. Suzanne and I considered not going but
decided there was no point in avoiding it. We arrived feeling uneasy and conspicuous.

For the past couple of months, I had been acutely
sensitive to being perceived as a bereaved parent. Little
things, trivial in themselves, forced themselves upon my
awareness; a lull in conversation as I approached, a forced
heartiness by an acquaintance upon meeting me, a surrep-
titious glance here, a failure to meet my eyes there. Additionally, a number of acquaintances had cut us socially;
invitations, except from close friends, had virtually ceased.
It took a while to register, but it finally dawned on me

that I was making a number of people uneasy. Since I was quite my usual ebullient, engaging self, I figured they weren't upset with me, they were having problems with the bereaved father.

It can be entertaining to stand aside and try to view yourself as others may see you, but I wasn't at all amused at seeing myself as a bereaved father. I wasn't comfortable in the role. I have played, to coin a phrase, many roles in my time—student, soldier, lover, teacher, and so forth—but I have never been bothered that people perceived me in those restricted capacities. I have never felt that in any important sense those roles defined me. I have always been more than met the eye. Now, however, I had a new role and it was causing me considerable difficulty.

The discomfort I detected in some people suggested to me that I might have fulfilled that ghastly fantasy that so many parents experience in those private, secret moments. It made me feel as though I'd somehow broken a taboo of my tribe, and for this violation I'd become a pariah. My presence made people uncomfortable because I was a reminder that their worst fears can come true. I'd become symbolic of their own vulnerability, a personified testimonial that dreadful things do happen. In my darkest moments, I felt like Oedipus: a thing pitied and despised, feared and unwelcome.

On the whole, though, we were made to feel welcome at the cocktail party. A number of people we had not seen since Peter's service made it a point to speak to us. We were kept busy talking from the moment we arrived. There was little of that stand-offishness you often encounter at affairs of this type, where you notice someone and see that he notices you, but each of you waits for the other to make the first move. Then, when you do meet, each registers delighted surprise, and you spend five minutes chatting about nothing.

Invariably, people would ask, "How are you doing?" and just as invariably I would answer, "Okay," by which I meant that I was surviving. I was coping. I was not physically ill nor was I falling apart psychologically—although there were those moments when I had my doubts. There really was no other answer to make. People want to hear that you're all right.

There was one man I couldn't stand, however, and when he asked me, I said, "Not so good." For a moment he looked horrified, and, before I knew it, he had launched into a discussion of his teenage son, which quickly turned into a diatribe. That certainly made me feel good. I excused myself as soon as I could. I rejoined Suzanne and we wandered about, listening, drinking, and snacking on canapés.

I felt disconnected, as though there were an invisible barrier between the others and myself that prevented real communication. I was an observer, not a participant. I listened to the chatter and laughter and felt I'd walked into the middle of Simon and Garfunkel's "Sounds of Silence": "people talking without speaking, people hearing without listening."

I was again reminded of my poor concentration when I joined a small group as someone was telling a joke. "These two penguins bump into Henry Kissinger on Second Avenue, and . . ." he began, and I mentally drifted off, thinking that once Peter and I had walked down Second Avenue together. I was tuned in sufficiently to laugh politely at the punch line, but I had no idea whether it was funny. From the way the others roared, I suppose it was. Suzanne and I had run out of steam by this point, so we quietly departed.

Suzanne told me on the way home that the only unpleasantness she'd experienced was sensing that a couple of people felt pity for her. One woman had said, "You poor dear." It was the tone, not just the words, Suzanne said, that conveyed the pity. It was infuriating. I agreed. Several times in the recent past I had encountered pity myself. Unlike sympathy or compassion, pity implies a lack of emotional involvement, a detachment, that makes the purveyor appear condescending. It makes you and your grief seem misunderstood. For a bereaved parent to feel himself the object of compassion is fine, to feel himself the object of pity is terrible.

In November, Sir Benjamin ate a ball, which got itself lodged in his intestine. It was a five-and-dime undersized soccer ball of Peter's, which Benjamin had unearthed amidst the endless clutter of our basement. Afterward, Suzanne said I'd better do something about the cellar before Benjamin found an even more dangerous item to eat. I've never understood how the basement became my responsibility, but I solved the problem with maximum ease for myself by simply making the cellar off limits to him.

At the time I didn't know he'd eaten the ball, but I knew he was sick, so I rushed him to our vet. He couldn't find anything wrong, even with x-rays, but agreed to keep him overnight for observation. With our luck, he wasn't taking any chances. The next day, as Benjamin showed clear signs of toxicity in his system and another x-ray indicated inflammation in his intestine, the vet operated. He called to say Benjamin was okay, but if we'd waited another day, he might have died. He also told me about the ball. He said he had saved it, in case I wanted a two-hundred-and-ninety-nine-dollar souvenir. It's wonderful having a vet with a sense of humor.

I discovered in the few days while Benjamin was in the hospital how much I missed the little creep. I also realized what a boon he had become. As soon as I got home from work, I had to take him for a walk—letting a bull terrier run loose is like playing Russian roulette with only one chamber empty. Then I had to feed him and, of course, play with him. As I usually got home before Suzanne, he gave me something to come .home to. Because of him, the house was not so empty. The other side of that coin, however, is that he began to assume an importance to me of worrisome proportions. But I figured it was a worthwhile risk.

In the months since Peter's death, Suzanne and I often talked about how we were feeling and how we were doing. Granted, she usually initiated these discussions, but I did respond. We were amazed to discover how similar our grieving patterns were. Often we seemed to be undergoing the same problems or experiencing the same mood at the same time. More important, though, by talking we found out where the other person was. We weren't always at the same place, but by talking we were able to support each other when help was needed. Talking encouraged us to be sensitive to the other person's needs. Sadly, we were atypical in this regard. For many of the bereaved couples we'd come to know, the lack of communication had become a serious problem in their marriages.

Even so, we had our problems. One of them began to surface at this time, possibly prompted by the holiday season drawing near. Suzanne said she needed to fill the void left by Peter's death. She mentioned various options: having another child, adopting one, or becoming foster parents. To me, each idea seemed worse than the other. I told Suzanne I would move out if her need for a child became stronger than her need for me. I couldn't bear the thought of another person in our house. The idea of undertaking that responsibility again and suffering that anxiety once more nearly drove me wild. We had come to an impasse. Fortunately, this conflict didn't become a serious problem at the time because we both realized it was too early in our bereavement to make a decision of this importance. But our differing needs lay between us.

We'd grown closer together the past few months, closer than we'd been for many years. We were both aware of this and talked about it. We agreed that we had a fairly good marriage. We'd had our crises and problems, but most of these either had been resolved or were being worked on. In the past a fair amount of the tension between us had concerned Peter. As a three-person household, we had been subjected to the stresses and strains of the infamous triangle. There had been shifting alliances, sometimes Peter and I, other times Peter and Suzanne, and often Suzanne and I.

I remember once at dinner, before Peter was in his teens, Suzanne asked me how I liked the meal. I responded by delivering a thunderous belch. Peter roared with laughter—he was an easy audience in those days.

Suzanne became furious and started taking me seriously to task. When Peter had himself under control, he said, "Aw, leave him alone, Mom," and looked at me conspiratorily, a couple of buddies united against Mrs. Etiquette.

But our system of alliances proved no more successful for keeping the peace in the long run than Bismarck's had. After Peter got older, his behavior caused tension between Suzanne and me, often because we disagreed about what our response should be. With his death this irritant was removed. Our relationship improved, which was good in that we were able to help one another; but it was bad in that there was a lot of guilt associated with our understanding of why it had improved. It was a high price to pay for matrimonial tranquility.

When Thanksgiving came, we were thankful for another bit of advice we had gotten at Compassionate Friends: vary your routine. Many bereaved parents had told us that they found the holidays nearly unbearable, and one way to make them tolerable was to do something different. We'd always celebrated Thanksgiving and Christmas at home, sometimes with other family members, other times with just the three of us.

This year we went with Jane and Michael to her cousin's in New Haven. It was a strange day and certainly different. Jane's cousin was terminally ill, a couple of other relatives failed to appear, and one of the party was a drunken bore. Jane and Michael couldn't get away fast enough, but it did the trick for us. Even though the meal was the traditional Thanksgiving one, the environment was so bizarre that I had little sense of the occasion. In fact, I felt as though I'd walked through the looking glass. Jane tried to apologize afterward, but we told her that, for us, the day had been a success. It had certainly taken our minds off ourselves.

We actually had two reasons for wanting to avoid a traditional Thanksgiving. Aside from the day normally being a happy family occasion for us, our last one with Peter had been a disaster. In fact, it hadn't been with Peter and that's what had made it one. He had been grounded for some serious infraction (which neither of us can now recall) the day before Thanksgiving. That night there was to be a party that apparently held special significance for him. We refused to lift the grounding, so that evening he slipped out of his window and took off. We made some phone calls but couldn't locate him or the party.

Thanksgiving morning, to our surprise, dismay, and anger, he had not returned. My mother was up for the holiday, and the three of us tried to proceed normally—but without much success. To his credit, Peter phoned during the day and agreed to come home that night. This incident resulted in his going to Dale.

We had a long talk with Peter in which we said that our relationship with him had reached a crisis. We felt that he was determined to fight us over every aspect of his upbringing. We admitted that we weren't always right, that we made mistakes, but we did discuss problems with him. We gave reasons and explanations for our decisions; decisions which were usually reached after examining the issues with him. As far as we could tell, he had little sense of responsibility toward himself or the household; he was consumed only with gratifying his immediate desires and avoiding anything that struck him as being unpleasant.

A household can function only with cooperation, we continued, and, as far as we were concerned, he wasn't cooperating. He wasn't studying; he continued to do dope; and he did his chores with poor grace, often having to be reminded that it was past the time to do them. We said we felt we were quite liberal—a couple of relatives even said we were too permissive—yet all we heard from him was about how arbitrary and strict we were.

I told him that my sense of responsibility as a parent, inseparable really from my sense of myself as a person, could not permit his flouting of the rules that we had laid down. Rules, I pointed out, that he had agreed to, however grudgingly.

"We can't make you obey or do those things we feel are best for you," I said. "This isn't a prison; we aren't going to use force—lock you in your room, for example. But we must have your cooperation or we can't continue as a family."

Suzanne stressed that for his own welfare he needed to find out why he was behaving the way he was. He needed help in doing this, she said, and suggested he see Dale. "You know him and you know you can trust him. Whatever you say to him will be treated confidentially, so you don't have to worry about his telling us. He has no ax to grind; his concern will be for you."

Peter agreed to see Dale at least for a few sessions and promised he would serve the remainder of his grounding. I told him that since he would see Dale, there would be no punishment for his recent conduct. I wanted him to understand that the problem was so serious that mere punishment was beside the point. "But just in case this is another of your con jobs, pal, understand this: you're not conning us, you're conning yourself. You can hurt us because we love you, but the only one you're screwing is yourself." It was the kind of statement that may not mean much to the other person, but it makes the speaker feel very self-statisfied. I was quite good at these.

In keeping with the holiday, I gave thanks that he was home, that he was safe, and that maybe a corner had been turned. I also gave thanks that I hadn't strangled him.

This current Thanksgiving, early in the morning, a solitary deer appeared at the back of the house. We were accustomed to seeing deer occasionally, but there had always been four or five of them together in the past—never a lone one and never one this close to our house. Suzanne felt its appearance wasn't fortuitous, that there was some meaning or symbolic significance involved. Given the circumstances of the previous Thanksgiving, it was as though Peter were signifying his forgiveness and contrition. She was deeply moved by its presence. I couldn't say anything, because I didn't want to destroy the good feeling it had given her. She later told a few bereaved friends about it and they were very responsive, for they, too, looked for signs. To me, the whole business had no deeper significance—though I had to admit that if there were something to it, the laugh would be on me. As it happened, the deer would appear again.

The traditional faculty party at school was held the Saturday before Christmas. In the past these parties were a lot of fun, and I had always enjoyed them. But this year I felt so drained after the first term, and so apprehensive about Christmas, that I couldn't face a throng of happy, boisterous merrymakers. I could face them, of course, but I saw no reason to put myself through the ordeal. A voice inside me said I was coddling myself. This voice had been bad-mouthing me most of my life. I told it to shut up, and I stayed home.

I loved Christmas above all holidays. One of my earliest and happiest childhood memories was of waking on Christmas morning, dawn not yet broken, and feeling the weight of my stocking and hearing the crinkling of the tissue-wrapped presents as I shifted my feet. The magic day had arrived, and after opening my stocking there would be a special breakfast, the tree with presents that Santa Claus had brought, and finally, dinner, with all its delicious goodies. I would have to wait for my parents to waken, but the anticipation was thrilling. I knew that the best present would be at the bottom, and I remember squeezing the stocking, trying to discover what it was. Later, I always made it a point to put a special present in Peter's stocking.

Suzanne and I decided that we would celebrate this Christmas in our traditional manner, but with a few changes. As usual, my mother would be with us, but this year my sister would come as well. Also, Jane and Michael were coming for breakfast. Suzanne insisted, however, that no stockings be hung. In her mind, this aspect of Christmas was most closely associated with Peter.

Nothing dramatic or untoward occurred, but it was a dreary day filled with disturbing memories. It was too soon to be able to recall with pleasure the earlier, happier Christmases with Peter. His absence haunted the house. We had fun with Jane and Michael at breakfast, exchanged presents and laughed a bit and made dinner, but it was hollow and meaningless. Another day to get through. A couple of Peter's friends stopped by later with presents. Suzanne had gotten them a little something, and their appearance meant a great deal to her. It meant something to me too: it was one of those countless reminders that Peter was dead. In those days, seeing his friends was more painful than pleasurable to me. Their presence emphasized his absence. As time passed, this became less of a problem, but in those early months it was one of the most sensitive aspects of my grieving.

Although we got through Christmas without any serious difficulties, the next few days found us in the throes of a deep depression. I suppose we'd prepared ourselves emotionally for Christmas and had been so busy the day itself that the full impact didn't hit until afterward. The letdown was more like a crashdown. Even the smell of the Christmas tree was depressing. The tree, probably because it symbolized the season, reminded me that one of my fantasies about Peter had been of spending Christmas with him and his children. I'd liked the idea of having grandchildren. I'd looked forward to telling them stories about their father—nice ones, such as the time we'd taught him to ride a bicycle or how he and I used to build castles with his wooden blocks: mine usually squat, unimaginative affairs; his, elegant, delicate structures. But now I wouldn't be able to and I felt sorry for myself. I felt cheated. I wanted to drag that goddamn tree, ornaments and all, out the door and chuck it into the woods. I couldn't even take pleasure in the presents I'd received, including the Godiva chocolates I normally lusted after.

Next to my feelings about Peter, the most depressing aspect of Christmas was the conviction that it would no longer hold its magic for me. After all, Christmas in its secular sense is for children. Those of us who feel that special sense of excitement about it as adults are really responding to the child in ourselves. In that sense, I felt certain that when Peter lost his adulthood, I lost my childhood.

When I say that nothing dramatic happened on Christmas day, I mean that there were no shocks. No presents or cards arrived for Peter, nor did any of us break down. There was one small occurrence, however, that had its share of drama for Suzanne. As I was preparing breakfast, I looked out the kitchen window and there again was a solitary deer. I didn't know if it was the same one, but it could have been; it looked to me, appropriately enough, like a young buck. I called Suzanne, who was dumfounded. The deer was about ten yards from the house, half-heartedly nibbling on something. At one point it looked up and gazed into the window out of which we were looking. Suzanne squeezed my hand as tears filled her eyes. We stood looking at it. I remained silent, as I knew that for her this was unquestionably a sign. To me it was still coincidence, if a slightly unnerving one. The deer finally wandered off into the woods, and I went to the stove and removed the bacon, which had cooked to a lovely crisp black.

New Year's Day was of no consequence; the holiday had never been important to us. But as I began writing 1980 on checks and correspondence, I was gripped by pain at the thought of leaving 1979, of leaving the year in which Peter had died. The new year seemed to signal that he was fading into the past, locked irretrievably into the year 1979. I felt as though I were being pulled away from him and that each year would take me farther away yet. He would gradually fade, his features and characteristics blurred by the passage of time. I'd already lost the sound of his voice; I couldn't hear his timbre or vocal inflections any more. Would I lose his other qualities as well? Would his other distinctive features shrink and dissolve until he was little more than a stick figure? Would time erode his outline until he became an abstraction, a vaguely remembered character from a book read long ago?

While I was watching the winter Olympics on television, I came to understand something about my grieving. Most of the time I was closed off from crying, from releasing the pain and grief I felt. My emotions had to be approached indirectly in order for the safety valves to be opened. I'd be watching something that touched me or that had high emotional intensity, and my eyes would tear. Unintentionally, my emotions would switch from the immediate stimulus to Peter, and I would nearly bawl.

That's what happened as I watched our Olympic hockey team defeat the Russians. It was one of those grand moments in sports when an underdog beats a heavily favored opponent. As the final seconds ticked away, the fans were screaming, the announcers were screaming, and I was bawling my eyes out. But my tears weren't for our team; they were for Peter, because he couldn't experience this glorious moment, because he would never experience any kind of moment again.

The same thing happened a few days later. As Eric Heiden received his fifth gold medal, I was touched by his extraordinary accomplishment. But the moment died in my heart when I realized that Peter would never know of Heiden's achievement. I was astounded that such inconsequential things could bring home so forcibly my sense of loss.

Aside from the anniversary of his death, the only other occasion we were dreading was Peter's birthday on February 20th. This would have been one of the big ones—his eighteenth. I was on a midwinter break from school, and Suzanne simply took the day off. We had agreed we'd spend the day together and decided to go to New York. We got there about midmorning, both of us feeling low and anxious about the day. We immediately bumped into Steve, from Suzanne's group. He had been to Peter's service and had come to the house afterward. I didn't know Steve very well, but he was one of those people you sense would be a friend if time and chance allowed. He had a dental appointment, but agreed to meet us for lunch at Fraunces Tavern.

One of my favorite pastimes was browsing through secondhand bookstores looking for bargains. Although the number of these stores has dwindled in recent years, there are still enough for me to indulge my habit. So we went downtown and spent the rest of the morning indulging.

As our living space had gradually decreased under the pressure of more and more books, Suzanne had made me promise that for every additional book that came into the house, an old one had to be removed. As with any agreement exacted under duress, this was one I felt morally obliged to circumvent whenever the occasion permitted. I guessed this was one of those occasions—because to my delight, and her chagrin, I had a shopping bag full by the time we headed for Wall Street.

Steve was waiting for us at the restaurant. The food was delicious, but the conversation left a lot to be desired. It wasn't bad at first, but then Suzanne and Steve started talking about Peter and the kinds of feelings Suzanne had been experiencing, and my food didn't taste so good any more. Although my appetite had improved from what it had been those first few days, I had soon discovered that nothing killed it faster than thinking or talking about Peter at mealtimes.

Suzanne was saying something about sadness and anger being inextricably bound together in her grief. As I toyed with a piece of shrimp, I realized I'd recently understood that about myself, although I hadn't thought the point through as clearly as she had. It made me remember how I'd often thought about Peter's accident, how I'd wondered if it had been his fault that he had died. Had he been hotdogging? Driving recklessly? Sometimes, in imaginary conversation with him, I'd ask quietly, with sadness and disappointment, "Oh, Peter. Why did you let it happen to you?" At other times I'd scream at him with fury and bitterness, "Look what you've done to your mother. And your grandmothers. And your friends. Look at how you've hurt us. Look at all the pain you've caused, you goddamn fool. Why didn't you listen? I tried to make you understand that you were fragile, vulnerable, mortal. Why didn't you do as I said and not as I did?"

The shrimp stuck in my throat. That final question took me by surprise—it had slipped in without invitation.

I supposed it was one that I'd avoided up to now, probably because of the guilt associated with it. The guilt seemed to work two ways. I'd done some wild, stupid things when I was young, yet I'd survived. On top of that, I had been fool enough to let Peter find out about some of them. Why hadn't I been more discreet? I might just as well have said to him, "Hey, kid. Look at how cool your old man was. Ever hear about the time I drove from Fort Devens, Massachusetts, to Bellport, Long Island, so stinking drunk I couldn't see straight? Not just tipsy or high, but falling-down drunk. Did it in six hours, before there were all these super highways. Never put a scratch on the car. Pretty good, huh?

"Or, how about this as a model for you? When I was a teenager, we had our own brand of 'chicken.' One of us would lie on the hood of a car with nothing to hold on to but the hood ornament—they were bigger in those days—and the game was to see how fast we could go before the guy chickened out. The drunker we were the braver we were. We hit some pretty high speeds. We almost lost a guy named Charlie one night. It scared us a bit, but what the hell, we were immortal then." I couldn't avoid the question that Suzanne's conversation had triggered: Was Peter pulling some stupid stunt like good old Dad? It's one of those forever questions because, of course, there's no answer. But you have to keep asking it.

Over coffee, I decided I'd have to do something about Suzanne's table conversation. Not today's lunch; that was understandable. But much of her dinner conversation, I realized, turned on the subject of death. As I'd already lost thirty-five to forty pounds, I'd soon waste away if this continued. I didn't object to talking about Peter or death; in fact, we did so often. It was her timing.

But as I thought about it, I realized I was bothered by her preoccupation with death. I supposed this was one of the ways in which we grieved differently. Suzanne had become fascinated with death. She read obituaries and was always ready to listen to death stories, particularly if they concerned children. Sometimes I felt her enjoyment wasn't complete until she'd passed these stories on to me. I knew I wasn't being fair, for she got no enjoyment from them, and they clearly filled some need in her. But they filled no need in me, especially at mealtime. I was up to my ears with Peter's death, and beyond that, I had no desire to pursue the subject.

We were compatible in our misery for the most part, but there were some differences. Suzanne was better at getting out her rage. In the early months especially, she screamed in her car when she was alone. She felt uninhibited in the privacy of her car; windows rolled up, she zipped along, screaming out her fury and frustration. Unfortunately, she also began driving recklessly for a period. I discovered that when she nearly put us into a tree one night because she was driving too fast on a twisting back road. It really was a close call.

Under cross-examination she admitted she'd been driving rashly for a month or so. "You know how anxious I get when you're just a little bit late," I said. "It's going to be even worse now, knowing you're driving like a maniac. You've got to cut it out. We've talked about our responsibility to each other, how we're more dependent on one another now. This isn't fair."

"When are you going to stop smoking?" she asked.

"Will you stick to the point?" I snapped exasperatedly.

I finally browbeat her into promising to reform her driving habits, with the assurance that I would stop smoking in the "near future."

We began to notice other differences in our grieving. Suzanne, like a number of bereaved parents, ceased to be bothered for the most part by petty, trifling matters. Compared with the enormity of Peter's loss, the mundane vexations of life were of no importance. I, on the other hand, had become even more irascible at the piddling annoyances of life. I suppose my reaction was that since I'd been subjected to the ordeal of Peter's death, I should be spared these minor irritations. Consequently, I had to guard against turning into a curmudgeon. I was also working hard at improving my ill-humored moods.

Another difference between us, but happily not a source of conflict, concerned religion. Peter's death regenerated Suzanne's religious impulse; it reaffirmed her belief in God. Although she began attending church occasionally, her real solace lay in the concept of God and an afterlife, with its promise of reunion, rather than in the institution of the church. Peter's death elicited no such response from me, but I was pleased that Suzanne had found comfort. She knew how I felt and put no pressure on me to accept her beliefs.

Suzanne still had her need for children, but dealing with that lay in the future. We knew how each other felt and understood that we faced a dilemma. We both hoped that time would see a change in one of us.

We understood that our ability to talk with each other, to share our feelings, was probably the single greatest aid in coping with Peter's death. But, given our differences, we also understood that in the end it came down to the individual himself. Support was helpful, necessary even, but we each had to come to terms with Peter's death on our own. Hearing other bereaved parents' stories was invaluable, but they were no substitute for doing your own death work. Supporting your mate may be essential, but it isn't sufficient. In the end, we are alone.

After lunch we walked around the Wall Street area. We went over to Trinity Church, where one of my ancestors is buried. I began to feel better as we strolled through the tiny, peaceful cemetery. That didn't surprise me, because I've always felt tranquil in cemeteries. There's something reassuring about them, as though seeing all those graves reminds us that we're not alone in our mortality. I wondered if there was a travel guide to the world's great cemeteries. I'd have to ask Jane and Michael, who've published several books in the travel genre.

Steve had to leave for work, so we headed back uptown. Seeing him had meant a lot, for he'd helped dispel some of the glumness we'd been feeling, despite my luncheon melancholy. Suzanne and I spent the rest of the afternoon window shopping, my bag of books growing steadily heavier. I considered asking her to carry it a while, but decided I'd better not push my luck. We went to the movies and got home about midnight. We'd gotten through the day and that was good enough.

FROM ABOUT the second or third month on, we had been constantly nagged by the question of how well we were doing. If we were upset and depressed, we wondered if we were coping adequately. Conversely, if we felt fairly good, we worried that we weren't confronting Peter's death properly. Even reassurance from people at Compassionate Friends didn't allay this concern.

For several months we had avoided using the road at night on which Peter had been killed. Daytime was no difficulty; it was just the night. We found the experience so painful and distressing that we'd decided this was one problem we weren't going to try to overcome at once. We had felt we weren't ready to deal with it. Then, having avoided the road for nearly eight months, I found myself on it one night quite by chance. I was nearly past the spot before I realized where I was. I was amazed to discover that I no longer felt that acute, stabbing pain. It was a bit upsetting, but not nearly as disquieting as before.

I didn't know if I'd handled the problem well or not. Had allowing myself the extra time done the trick, or had I pushed the problem so deeply inside myself that I was no longer in touch with the feelings associated with it? I told Suzanne about my experience and my misgivings. Within a few days she used the road at night herself. Her reaction was much the same as mine. Also, we both felt a little guilty that we could use the road without feeling the old intense pain.

"I'm not going to let it bother me," Suzanne said. "I've done all I'm capable of; I've dealt as openly and directly with Peter's death as I can. I'm either in good shape or I'm not—only time will tell. But I think this proves something we heard at Compassionate Friends: you don't have to deal with all aspects of your child's death at once; you can delay some things."

I agreed. In fact, I began to suspect that my being on that road that night was not so accidental after all. Perhaps I had been ready, and taking the road had been my way of showing that to myself. It was a comforting thought.

I was also comforted when I realized that the intensity of my pain had recently dulled somewhat. Nonetheless, Peter's death continued to impinge upon virtually everything we did. For instance, when Suzanne and I went to see the movie *Superman,* a piece of fluff really, I was deeply moved by two scenes.

The first occurs when Superman, still a teenager, tests his developing powers by racing a speeding train. Typical of so many teenagers and certainly characteristic of Peter, he overreaches: he gets to a crossing at the same time as the train, and only by a desperate, superhuman leap does he avoid being hit. Peter often raced trains, in a manner of speaking, so I supposed it had been only a matter of time before he met one at a crossing.

The second scene begins with Lois Lane in a crashed helicopter dangling precipitously on the roof edge of a tall building. Clark Kent races to find a place to change. He heads for a phone booth, but it's a modern half-booth —he can't change there. With growing desperation, he races across the street. He sees an alley or a deserted cul-de-sac and runs toward it. The helicopter lurches— only seconds left before Lois crashes to the ground. Even before he reaches the alley, Kent removes his tie and starts to unbutton his shirt, which opens enough for us to see the *S* emblazoned on his chest. We realize his desperation; he's in danger of blowing his cover, so totally committed is he to saving Lois. We also realize when we see that *S* that Superman is going to save her.

By this point my eyes were so tear-filled I could barely see the screen. If only I could have saved Peter. If only I'd awakened sooner and flown up the street and caught him before he hurtled into the telephone pole. But I had no *S* on my chest. So I sat in that darkened theater, crushed by my powerlessness.

As we drove home, I thought of the last movie that Peter and I had seen together. It wasn't difficult to remember, because I seldom went to movies nowadays. We'd seen *Close Encounters,* and the experience had been a good one even though we'd disagreed about the quality of the film. He'd thoroughly enjoyed it, while I'd thought it was distractingly flawed. We'd talked about it afterward. I'd tried to give him my views without making them a putdown of something he'd liked. For once I'd shown some sense in debating an issue with him. I hadn't tried to convince him that my position was the correct one, since the experience, values, and judgment that made up my critical sensibility were more developed than his.

I could remember, as a boy in my late teens, being shot down by adults whose polemical ordnance was too powerful for me. I couldn't compete with them on their level of sophistication. They were little more than intellectual bullies, and as an adult I was aware of this characteristic in myself. I'd had no problems with my students in this regard, but I sometimes overwhelmed Peter. I suppose I expected too much of him. In any case, on this occasion we'd had a good exchange. I'd managed to be honest without being offensive. I valued memories of this sort.

Another good conversation with Peter was brought to mind when a student came to me with a problem concerning his girfriend. Shortly after Peter had switched to Wilton High School in his sophomore year, two lovely young things had appeared at the door one day inquiring for him. Forthwith, he and I had a discussion about sex.

Once, when he had been between three and four, he had given us his version of the birds and the bees. He had said that the daddy cat looked down the mommy cat's throat, and if he saw an egg in her stomach, he planted his seed. I assumed that his understanding had progressed in the intervening years beyond this suggestively oral conception of sex, but I was equally sure his knowledge was as spotty as mine had been at his age.

I told him I thought we'd better have a chat about sex now that he was launching himself socially. His reply was noncommital, but his mien suggested definite interest.

The thrust of our talk concerned VD and pregnancy, but we discussed attitudes as well.

I told him he could approach sex in either of two ways. He could treat it as a physical, animalistic rutting, be concerned only with his own gratification, indifferent to who the girl was. Or, he could treat sex as an extension of a deep feeling he had for someone and make the experience a giving, sharing, loving one. I strongly recommended the latter as the more rewarding.

"This sounds like one of your lectures," he said, beginning to look bored. "I don't want to get married, I just want some fun. Why do I need to worry about all that stuff?"

"Just listen a minute, will you please? I'm talking about attitude. Do you see the girl as someone to use, or someone to share with? As far as any particular girl is concerned, ask yourself if you like her as a person. Do you have common interests? Would you be proud to be seen with her? Or, are you simply attracted by her body? Remember, just because you're a male doesn't mean you have to nail every girl who waggles her butt at you."

"Did you ask those questions when you started taking Mom out?"

This wasn't going right. "We're not discussing your mother at the moment, if you don't mind. But, as a matter of fact, we'd established a pretty strong relationship before we slept together. Furthermore, your mother wasn't a butt-waggler."

"Okay. But how can you know all this if you've just met a girl?" he scoffed.

"That's difficult," I admitted. "What I mean is, if you

have sex with a girl, do it because you like her, not just to get your ashes hauled."

He laughed. " 'Ashes hauled.' Where'd you hear that one?"

"In a locker room probably."

"What other ways of saying it do you know?"

I had his attention now. "Look, there's a couple of other things I want to say before we get into that. What do you know about preventing pregnancy?"

"Oh, there's all sorts of stuff," he said, somewhat uncomfortably.

"Such as?"

"Girls use the pill . . . and there's rubbers."

"The pill's pretty good, but rubbers are unreliable. Don't count on them. And remember this: the last thing you want at your age is to make a girl pregnant. You have an obligation as much as she does to make sure she doesn't. If she should, it would be your problem as well as hers. Just be careful."

He knew next to nothing about VD, so I told him the more common signs to look for, and that, if he ever found any, even if he didn't speak to us, he should get to a doctor or clinic at once—and warn the girl he had been with. He said he would, and added, "Let's hear some more words for screwing."

After his death I found out from a close friend of his that he hadn't died a virgin. From his friend's description it sounded as though he'd chosen the second option we'd discussed. I was pleased on both counts.

Recalling this conversation also induced some feelings that were not so pleasing. I had the sense that our efforts to raise and teach Peter had been wasted, since he had had so little opportunity to put*that training into practice. Intellectually, I realized that our love, guidance, and teaching had had immediate value, but emotionally I couldn't afford the depressing feeling of waste, since the real goal of such endeavors had been to prepare him for adulthood.

I realized that a certain amount of our emotional investment in Peter had been in terms of his future. I remembered taking great pleasure in thinking that many of the experiences to which we'd exposed him would be ones on which he'd look back fondly. I supposed this was important to me because of the value I attached to my own early memories. Often, during our summer in Montana, for example, we'd eaten trout that Peter had caught in the Flathead. He'd cleaned them as well, for his mother had drawn the line at performing such messy work. As she was a strong supporter of the women's movement, we started calling her the Frontier Feminist. He'd gotten a big kick out of that, but his greatest pleasure had been our enjoyment of the fish. "How do you like the trout, Dad?" was an oft-asked question at mealtime.

That summer, in fact, had been filled with memorable events for him. One day he and I had been shooting BBs at plastic soldiers in a dry riverbed when a meteor had passed overhead. Except for a whooshing sound it had been silent, but brilliantly lit, like a minuscule sun shooting across the sky. I'd thought it was only a few hundred feet in the air, but it must have been much higher for I heard later that it crashed in New Mexico or Arizona. Peter couldn't wait to tell his mother. Even at the time, part of my enjoyment had derived from thinking of what a wonderful memory this would be for him. I suppose it was, for seven years.

Related to the sense of waste was the realization that Peter belonged to the past. From about the eighth or ninth month on, this feeling began to intrude itself more and more forcibly upon me. Perhaps that indicated a greater acceptance of his death on my part, or, more likely, a greater adjustment to it.

Parents think of their children in terms of the future; indeed, to think of them *as* the future. We certainly did. When Peter goes to college, when Peter gets married, when . . . In this sense he was to be our future. But now, I thought, he's the past. He's dated. Watching the news one evening about the hostages in Iran, I realized that Peter had been dead before they were taken. He was pre-hostage. He belongs only to the past, as does F.D.R., Shelley, and the Reformation. He's historical, in that sense. He's locked in time, his period established, while I'm still fluid, my span not yet fixed.

Sometimes, when I thought of the shortness of Peter's life, it was as if I were viewing it in time-lapse photography: I saw him develop from an infant to a seventeen-year-old in a matter of seconds. Such a short life emphasizes the tragedy of potential unrealized. I told Suzanne what I'd been feeling, and she'd had similar thoughts. She remarked how unnatural it was. Indeed, the recognition that our son belonged to the past went against something both instinctive and learned in us. It brought back the old feeling that the world was out of joint.

The winter trimester at school was nearly over, which meant that the wrestling season was nearing its end. I hadn't attended a match all year, although the coach and several wrestlers had often informed me of upcoming contests. I even had a schedule in my desk, but somehow I kept forgetting. It finally dawned on me that I wasn't forgetting, but avoiding. I'd never fully realized how much I'd invested in Peter's athletics, especially his wrestling, until that moment. I also understood with a clarity I'd never had before another reason why his doping had been so deeply disturbing to me. For, unsurprisingly, as his doping increased, his athletic participation decreased. Athletics had not only been an important part of my youth, but it also had formed a strong bond in my relationship with Peter.

When he'd been four, the two of us played football each Sunday up to the Sunday before Christmas, when we had the championship game. We played tackle, and even then he threw himself into the game with fearless disregard. Once, when I tackled him near the end of a game, he landed with a thump and began crying. I was sure he wasn't really hurt, so I hiked the ball to him for the next play. He just stood there, holding the ball and crying. "Hurry up," I said. "Time's running out." He hesitated a moment and came charging at me. He made a good gain before I brought him down. He jumped up at once, the tears gone. I tried to teach him that some things are fun only if you're willing to work hard and take a few lumps. I didn't always let him win, either. In fact, we were tied going into the championship game.

It had snowed the night before, so I had to shovel off our field while my opponent sat in a warm kitchen discussing strategy with his mother. It was a close game, but he won in the last few seconds despite a heroic goal-line stand on my part. Suzanne said afterward, "Thank God. I couldn't have stood another defeat." It turned out that whenever he lost, he was absolutely furious and complained bitterly to his mother.

I coached the middle-school team when Peter was in seventh grade. Most of my players were eighth graders, but I had a handful of seventh graders, Peter among them, on the first team. I tried to walk that delicate line of impartiality with Peter, treating him as I did the others. If anything, I erred on the side of being tougher. For most of the season I used him only on defense. In one of our last games, when an opposing player was making mincemeat out of our running game, I'd yelled, "Get in there, Mitchell, and block that number sixty-four!" I heard one of the kids on our bench say, with a mixture of awe and disbelief, "Wow! Did you hear that? He called his son by his last name." After watching Peter level number sixty-four with a beautiful open-field block, I realized I should have started him on offense as well.

He was a fearless, hard-nosed player. As a coach I loved it; as a father I hated it. Suzanne arrived at the end of our first home game just in time to see her son stretched out on the field, a doctor bending over him. Peter had taken on a huge running back single-handedly—a ninth grader, I found out later—and stopped him. The game was well lost, only seconds remained, and most players would have dogged it. Fear and pride were swirling through me as the doctor examined him. He was okay; he'd simply had his bell rung rather soundly. As I helped him to his feet, his mother gave me a look that's conventionally described as "withering." We had a spirited discussion that night about the virtues of football. Suzanne reluctantly agreed to his continued playing.

Peter's football playing was a source of pride to me, more for his attitude than for his accomplishment, although there was plenty of that, too. In the eighth grade, he scored the only touchdown in a game against Rye on a fifty-five-yard run from scrimmage—the kind of thing a kid dreams about. I missed it because I was scouting the varsity's next opponent. I've regretted that deeply. But I told him how proud I was, and I'm glad of that.

I was even prouder of his wrestling. It wasn't only a question of his being good, which he was, but it also had to do with the nature of the sport. Unlike team sports, in wrestling you're on your own, vulnerable, exposed; you have no teammates to hide behind, no one else to blame for defeat. Also, because of the problem of making weight, wrestling requires greater self-discipline and self-denial than any other schoolboy sport with which I'm familiar. I quickly realized the depth of my emotional involvement in his wrestling when I nearly threw up after his first match. He won, but the tension was nauseating. As his wrestling career progressed, I improved, but his matches remained nerve-wracking nonetheless.

While still in eighth grade, he wrestled in a varsity match. Being the lightest weight, he wrestled first. I could tell from his frozen expression and stiff movements that he was nearly petrified with apprehension. Once his match began, however, he was fine and he won, gaining three points for King. We eventually won the match by three points. All the winning wrestlers contributed to the overall victory, of course, but to my mind, it was Peter's victory.

In his ninth-grade year, Big Peter, Suzanne, and I

accompanied him to a tournament in New York. He was on dope by this point. He wrestled his heart out, but lack of proper training and conditioning took its toll. By the third period he was out of steam. He didn't quit, but he didn't have enough left. He lost a couple of vital points and that was the match. As sorry as I was for him, I felt hurt and let down, personally injured.

The abandon, even recklessness, with which he threw himself into athletics was in keeping with his behavior generally. He'd gotten his first bicycle when he was five. It was too big for him and, even with blocks strapped onto the pedals, he couldn't brake properly. His method for stopping was to run the bike into a hedge or some other handy object. He was constantly bruised and scratched, but that didn't keep him off the bike.

By the time he was six, we had a junior Evel Knievel on our hands. One day he was showboating, evidently, when he went over the handlebars onto a graveled sidewalk. His face was a mess. In his lip was embedded a pebble, which I thought at first was a tooth. While Suzanne got the car, I felt in his mouth to make sure there was no other debris on which he might choke. I was fine as long as there was something to do, but once we got to the emergency room, I felt sick with apprehension. For the first time, I experienced actual fear at his vulnerability—and his overreaching. He received another lecture in an ongoing series about safety and caution. Within a few days, of course, he was again popping wheelies despite our warnings.

When he was ten or eleven, he fell down an unusually steep embankment—the slope must have been nearly seventy degrees—in the woods by a friend's house. Buried under leaves near the bottom of the hill were some large chunks of concrete, on which he ripped his knee open. The skin and tissue were hanging loose, and I could see bone through the blood. I hoisted him over my shoulder and started up the hundred or so feet to the top of the hill. That climb damn near killed me. By the time I got to the top, I thought I'd need emergency attention myself.

Apparently they'd been playing Robin Hood, and Peter had been in hot pursuit of the Sheriff of Nottingham—he was too young to have risked injury chasing Maid Marian —when he'd taken his tumble. Luckily, there were no lasting consequences of his fall, aside from a nasty scar. That is, no consequences for him; for us it was a different matter. He was the only kid who fell, because he was the only one who pushed the limits. This incident, on top of many others, indicated that we'd simply have to adjust to having an overreacher on our hands. We tried to strike a balance between common sense and overprotectiveness in our handling of him, hoping that his athleticism would save him from serious injury until maturity calmed him down.

Thinking back to these and other childhood escapades of Peter's was often a source of pleasure to me during this period of my grieving. They not only harkened back to a period when we were very close, but they also represented perils successfully avoided. Even in the context of what ultimately happened, they became happy, comforting memories, not simply ominous forerunners of what was to come.

That's not to say I didn't also see them as parts of the behavioral pattern which led inexorably to his final catastrophe. They were harbingers of his absolute, total, unqualified vulnerability. I don't think he'd have been able to believe it himself, that this had happened to him. Of all the kids in his class, only he had died. It had *actually* happened to him. Would he have been embarrassed that it had happened on a puny moped, rather than a powerful motorcycle? I was obsessed with wondering what had gone through his mind in that last second of his life. Had that as-yet-poorly-understood center of our being informed the organism that it was going to perish? Had he screamed his life away in abject terror? Crushing, unanswerable questions.

Peter's recklessness had continued to the end. There's a park in our town which has an enormous weeping beech. The kids refer to it as the monkey tree. With its drooping, twisted branches, it's great climbing tree. Several of Peter's friends have told us that it was amazing, even frightening, to watch him swinging about in it. He would attempt stunts that none of the others would dare try.

One night, according to Ricky, he and Peter and another boy were at the park, completely skulled. Peter was performing his usual routine in the tree, when he suddenly came sailing out of it and landed flat on his back. The sound was sickening, Ricky said. Peter just lay there, unmoving. They rushed over to him. "Are you dead?" one of them asked. "I don't think so," came a faint reply from the still form. Fortunately, there was a resurrection on that occasion.

Undeniably, our most unpleasant memory of Peter concerned his doping. I didn't know when he began, but by some point in his ninth-grade year the signs were clearly evident. His studies, which had never been strong, dropped off; his interest in athletics declined—for example, in the spring he switched from lacrosse to tennis, a sport that had been a joke at King for years; rock music and concerts became his passion; and an attitude of apathy and passive resistance developed. Yes, all the evidence was there, but I wouldn't allow myself to see it. I knew that he was doping but I didn't know. It was too threatening.

I've never understood fully why he doped. Once you remove the generalities such as it's cool and it's fun, as well as such intangibles as peer pressure, you're still left with the question of why this individual turned to drugs while others didn't. We bear some of the responsibility. Alcohol (a drug by any other name is just as deadly) had been an important part of our lives for a good many years. I, in particular, had a problem with it, so much so that I'd gone on the wagon and had been dry for three years prior to his death.

Additionally, Peter had always admired older kids. Invariably, he had been impatient with the limitations his current age had imposed upon him. Although this characteristic is common to many adolescents, I believe he felt it more keenly than most, and it made him highly susceptible to attempting more than he could handle.

Aside from external influences, I suspect his doping was due partly to his audacious, rash nature. Here was another challenge, made more attractive by adult condemnation, that had to be answered. Here was another opportunity to try the sharp edge of experience. Also, the illegality of dope and the risk inherent in using it were not exactly restraints upon him.

After we could no longer ignore that he was doping,

and had ourselves failed to dissuade him from the practice, we had him see a local doctor who'd had success helping kids with drug problems. Unhappily, he wasn't able to help Peter. It may well have been a case of Peter's refusing to meet him halfway. We never once sensed that Peter understood the danger of drugs or how adversely they were affecting him. Our advice and warnings were relegated to the realm of parental propaganda. Consequently, Suzanne and I felt angered and betrayed, and no doubt Peter felt put upon and bullied. His doping had become a divisive factor in our relationship, and all three of us were the losers for it.

CHAPTER

12

IN APRIL, Dr. Mitchell died from a massive heart attack. Big Peter made the arrangements with the same funeral home we'd used for Peter. When we got there we discovered that Dr. Mitchell was in the same room as well. At first, both Mrs. Mitchell and Suzanne were horrified, but once in the room, they were glad that he was sharing the same spot as Peter. As I walked over to Big Peter, I thought, *"You poor bastard, losing both your father and your son within nine months almost to the day."* I looked at him closely, convinced that such a harrowing occurrence must have marked him physically.

The next day we attended the funeral service. It was a Mass, and so different from Peter's that I had little difficulty coping with it. Suzanne was lost in her own reflections. She felt that Dr. Mitchell was lucky, because he was the first to be reunited with Peter. He had been Peter's only grandfather—despite a plethora of grandmothers—and they'd been very close. She recalled the two of them watching cartoons on television, laughing their heads off at the silly stuff. She thought of the time, when Peter was small, that she'd seen them walking to the village of Old Greenwich to buy a paper, Peter talking a mile a minute, Dr. Mitchell mostly silent, occasionally nodding his head to the nonstop chatter.

She remembered how incredibly sad Dr. Mitchell had been at Peter's death. It had been impossible for him to talk about it. Even looking at pictures of Peter had been too painful. Shortly after our return from Colorado, we'd gone out to dinner with them. Suzanne had brought along some pictures we'd taken at the cemetery. Mrs. Mitchell had taken them to have duplicates made, but Dr. Mitchell hadn't wanted to see them. We'd had a pleasant dinner, but there'd been little mention of Peter, even though his presence had been almost tangible. After Dr. Mitchell had died, she told us that he'd never recovered from Peter's death.

For us, but especially for Suzanne, the worst part was going to the cemetery. It was the first time since we'd buried Peter that we'd been to one, except for that stroll through Trinity Church's. Suzanne was thankful that Peter wasn't buried there, that we wouldn't have to go to his grave in this public manner with all these people, some of whom we didn't even know. She also felt a little sad that Peter, being a Mitchell, wasn't buried there too.

Mrs. Mitchell and Big Peter insisted that we return to her house afterward. There would be just the family and a few old friends. It was so strange talking with that part of Peter's family without his being there, without anyone asking how he was, what he was doing in school, comparing him with his cousins, remarking how grown-up, or how dreadful, he looked with his scraggly beard and mustache.

I started having another of those displacements. I felt dislocated, as though I were in someone else's dream, vaguely familiar with my surroundings but ignorant of the context or significance of what I observed. I was going through the expected motions, but the texture, the atmosphere, was shadowy, almost chimerical. Reality was just beyond my grasp, illusive and insubstantial. Pain couldn't touch me in this psychological limbo.

Throughout the entire ritual, but especially at the Mitchells', Suzanne felt a strong sense of being a surrogate. Although we would have attended under any circumstances, she sensed she was standing in for Peter. She also sensed that it was important to Mrs. Mitchell, Big Peter, and his sister, Diane, that we were there. Judging from their warmth and consideration, I was sure she was right. I suspect that for them, Dr. Mitchell's death was as inextricably bound with Peter's as it was for us.

While at the Mitchells', I noticed a stack of Mass cards on a table in the hall. They reminded me of the letters of condolence we'd received at the time of Peter's death. I couldn't remember what we'd done with them. A week or two later, while rummaging through a closet, I came across the shoe boxes in which we'd put them. Aside from that day at the Mitchells', I hadn't thought of them in months.

From about the third day on, they had come pouring in, and a steady stream had continued for several weeks. We started counting each day's haul, as though the sheer volume held some significance. It was as if a grotesque equation obtained, in which the number of letters received equaled the importance and value of Peter.

We found reading these letters very rough going. Suzanne often read correspondence aloud, but when she tried to read the first few letters to me, she started crying so much I couldn't make head or tail of them. Each was an ordeal to read, yet each gave comfort. Each heightened our sense of injury, of loss, yet each warmed and sustained us. We were glad to get them: given the first circumstance, we needed the second one.

Suzanne answered a few of the letters but found it so arduous she soon desisted. I tried a couple with no better success myself. I couldn't find the words to express the emotions I was feeling, no doubt because I was in such emotional turmoil. We worried about not answering them, until several friends told us not to be foolish; people don't expect responses to notes of this kind.

When I discovered the shoe boxes, my curiosity got the better of me, and I tried reading a couple of the letters. That was a mistake. They brought back, with all the attendant horror, that ripping, searing pain of the early days. In my distress, I felt as if I'd gone back in time some nine or ten months. All the assuagement and progress of the intervening time had been stripped away, my feelings again raw and exposed. For a brief period I experienced a suffocating anguish of such intensity that I felt trapped by the limitations of my physical being, as though I had to get outside myself in order to find release, a surcease of torment. I was like a claustrophobic trapped in an elevator between floors, hysteria building at his insoluble predicament. I put the letters away. I wasn't ready yet—not by a long shot.

In one of the boxes was a small white envelope with no writing on it. Inside was a lock of Peter's hair about which I had also forgotten. Suzanne had asked the undertaker to cut off a couple of locks, after everyone had left that Friday. Big Peter hadn't wanted one, but his mother had. I hadn't cared one way or the other. Finding the lock of hair was of no moment, because I couldn't have felt any worse than I did after reading the letters. But it did have an effect on some part of my mind, for that night I dreamed of Peter for the first time since his death.

Beginning with that first night after his death, I'd been faced with a dilemma at bedtime. On the one hand, I was worried that I wouldn't be able to sleep, and, on the other, that if I did sleep I would dream about him. For the most part I'd had no difficulty sleeping. As there had been no more than a dozen nights at most when sleep had eluded me, I had had no complaints on that score. More worrisome was the question of the kinds of dreams I would have if I did dream about him.

I was afraid that I'd have nightmares, that my sense of guilt and rage, especially the guilt, would give me horrible dreams. More disturbing, however, was the fear that I'd dream he was alive and, in that state between sleep and wakefulness, believe he *was* alive and that his death had itself been only a nightmare. I could imagine the momentary surge of joy I'd feel before reality returned to crush me again.

Happily, my dreams that night after finding the lock of hair did not measure down to my worst expectations. I had a nightmare in which I was tracked down and surrounded by a platoon of German soldiers whose one objective in life, it seemed, was to kill me. They had me trapped and, unlike so many dreams, there was no escape. They raised their rifles to fire and I experienced absolute terror. I don't remember what happened next, but my dream changed. I was going down some unfamiliar stairs, and several people were standing by the railing. One of them was Peter. I was really only conscious of his beautiful hair, and, as I passed down by him, I reached out and touched it and said, "Hi, kiddo." I experienced a warm, happy feeling as I did so. I know there was more to the dream, but that's all I remember.

Fortunately, there was no confusion between fantasy and reality as I awakened. I was still in the thrall of the dream, however, and was consumed by the terror of being trapped and shot, as well as by the warmth of my contact with Peter. At first the terror predominated, but as the day passed it faded, replaced by the feeling of happiness at experiencing Peter. Unlike most of my dreams, the inherent sensations lasted for several days. Nonetheless, I have yet to dream of him again.

Suzanne, on the other hand, has often dreamed of him. Her dreams have been a mixture of good and bad, but mostly good, with a dominant pattern running through them. She'll dream about something apparently unrelated to Peter, when out of nowhere he'll suddenly appear. She knows he's dead, and she's both shocked and baffled by his return. Sometimes he looks perfectly normal, other times he seems sick or injured. Invariably she asks him what he's doing here; he's supposed to be dead. Occasionally he won't respond, but usually he tells her, with an expression that suggests she's making a big deal out of nothing, that he's all right. As overjoyed as she is to see him, she still knows he's dead but can't reconcile the contradiction. Generally, she has a good feeling upon awakening. As a paradigm of wish fulfillment, her dreams are classics, and several of our bereaved friends have had ones of a similar nature.

A different problem that harries many bereaved parents is what to say when asked by people, who don't know them, if they have children. This usually happens in a social setting of some sort, and the obvious temptation is not to mention your dead child in order to avoid interjecting a gloomy note into the proceedings, as well as the understandable hesitation of getting into such a personal area with strangers. Even though I was having problems with my role as a bereaved parent, this facet of it gave me no difficulty. Certainly I was more comfortable if people didn't know I was a bereaved parent, but I couldn't disown Peter and his brief existence.

Suzanne, however, denied Peter a couple of times when asked this question—and paid dearly for it. One of her duties at the health department was running a program at a senior citizens' center. She was chatting with an old man there one day, when he asked if she had any children. She said no. Suzanne looks a good ten years younger than her age—possibly from living so long with a buoyant, carefree chap like me—so the old man proceeded to lecture her that a young, healthy woman like her should have children. He went on at great length and finally she began to cry. She told him about Peter, and, needless to say, the poor old guy was terribly embarrassed and highly apologetic. Suzanne felt miserable and the incident preyed upon her for days.

Another time, at a conference in Hartford, Suzanne was talking with a couple of women when the subject of children arose. They were both mothers, and one of them asked Suzanne if she had children, and again she answered no. The women began talking about the problems of motherhood and one of them said to Suzanne, "You won't fully understand this, not being a mother, but. . . ." Suzanne was devastated. She vowed then and there that the cock would never crow a third time.

I suspect that one reason why Suzanne and other bereaved parents answer in the negative is because the question "Do you have?" is present tense, and you feel so strongly that you no longer do that you say no. Quite obviously you don't. Your child *is* no more. He's past tense. It's the logical answer to make.

Aside from avoiding unpleasant situations, Suzanne soon found that a positive reason for answering in the affirmative was the rewarding experience that might ensue. She was chatting with a woman at a health fair one day and mentioned that she'd lost her son. The woman said that she had lost hers ten years ago. She told Suzanne that she seldom spoke of him. But she did so then. It was a brief conversation, but as they parted, the woman said, "We've only talked for a few minutes and I'm sure I'll never see you again, but I'll never forget you or this moment. Thank you so much." As far as we're concerned, the discomfort or awkwardness that may arise from acknowledging Peter to strangers is small, compared with the gratification an incident like this can provide.

As Peter was constantly in my thoughts, I didn't need external stimuli to remind me of him. But the reminders were there, and none were sadder or more evocative than his treasured possessions, most of which were lodged in his room. We never seriously considered dismantling it, but we worried about turning it into a shrine. By *shrine* we had in mind that kind of twisted veneration that attempts to freeze time at the moment of a person's death, his possessions kept inviolate awaiting his return. We had no intention of pulling a Miss Havisham, however. We made it into a guest room, but we kept it essentially as he'd left it, and we still referred to it as "Peter's room."

Over the months we'd given a number of things to his close friends, as well as some old toys to younger relatives, such as his electric trains to his cousin Tommy. Although Suzanne was by no means trying to dispose of his belongings, she was more generous than I in offering them to others. Aside from those items we clearly intended to keep, we had some lively arguments over this issue.

From the time he was little, Peter loved fishing. Over the years he'd accumulated a lot of fishing gear. He had a fine assortment of flies, many of which he'd made himself. We'd joined an outdoor book club for him, and he had a collection of books that covered all aspects of fishing. When we'd given them to him, I'd thought of how much pleasure they'd give him as long as his interest in fishing continued. And indeed they had. I had no interest in the sport myself, so I considered giving them away. It made me feel uncomfortable, however, even disloyal, since he'd enjoyed them so much. I told myself I was being absurd. I shouldn't let it bother me, because books and fishing are things of life, and Peter was no longer a thing of life. But I've kept them anyway.

When Peter returned from Atlanta that time, he came back with not only the Babe Ruth ball signed by Hank Aaron, but with another one, signed just by Aaron. After Peter died, I gave the balls back to Big Peter, but he insisted I keep the one with Aaron's signature. I value the ball today, not so much for old Hank, but for what that ball meant to Peter and for Big Peter's gesture.

Thinking about that ball one day made me realize that Peter's possessions had become an objective correlative for all that he meant—and means—to us. They emphasized the magnitude of what he'd lost himself, not simply our grief for what we'd lost. That was another component that made up the mechanism of our bereavement. In the early months I'd been more conscious of the pain I felt at my loss; now I was grieving for what he'd lost. Death had deprived him of the capacity to enjoy, to experience, to grow. I realized that what hurt so much now was the knowledge that he hadn't wanted to die and that the normal span of years had been denied him. It was the idea of how much he would miss that ate at me. For me it was another way of comprehending the tragedy of his untimely death.

Toward the end, Peter had begun to pull himself together. There were some signs, some indications—admittedly far from conclusive—that he'd finally realized where his own best interests lay. Assuming this to be the case, I felt both saddened and gladdened. It was sad to think that he died before he could enjoy the benefits of his reformation, but it was pleasing to consider how much better he may have felt about himself.

Several of his friends told us that he'd really cut down on his doping during the summer. Of course, they may simply have been telling us what they figured we'd want to hear. I don't know. It's often difficult to know if people are telling you the truth—almost as difficult as knowing if you're telling yourself the truth. I was inclined to believe them, however, because, looking back, I could see that his attitude had certainly improved. He was a more pleasant individual to be around, and that June we'd had a brief conversation that suggested a new maturity.

He'd told me about a man my age who worked at the same garage he did. In most of the gas stations in our area, kids are hired to do the gas pumping. This man had no skills, so pumping gas was one of the few jobs he could handle. Peter said he realized now what we'd been saying to him about the importance of school. School would give him options: he could be a mechanic or short-order cook if that was what he wanted to be, but how pitiful if those jobs were the only ones he could perform. This man had opened his eyes, he said. He told me he intended to buckle down to his studies that coming fall. I said I was glad to hear it and even managed to refrain from saying, I told you so. Whether or not he could have followed through, I would have liked him to have had the chance at least.

I was certainly pleased that he'd come to understand a point we'd made to him in the past, but a little bitter that he couldn't simply have taken our word for it. Thinking about this incident, I realized that I was resentful that Peter hadn't taken my advice as often as I had wished. I guess I'd expected him, like Hamlet, to carry a tablet, a notebook, so he could jot down the pithy advice I gave him and later incorporate it into his daily life. Revere each pearl I cast before him.

A piece of advice we'd heard repeated at a number of of Compassionate Friends meetings was not to make any important decisions for at least a year after your child's death. There's nothing magical about this period of time, but it is a convenient milestone to use, for it implies the passage of a sufficient amount of time for the bereaved to have overcome his shock and to have gained a needed perspective. Naturally, I didn't follow this advice any more than Peter followed mine.

For years I had wanted to write, but various factors, external and internal, had prevented me from doing so. I had started a novel some years ago but never finished it. For one thing, I didn't have the energy to write after a full day's work. More important, however, were the psychological factors. I was hampered on the one hand by a sense of inadequacy and fear of failure, and on the other, by a refusal to allow myself the pleasure and satisfaction of accomplishment.

Within a few months of Peter's death, I began examining myself and realized that I wanted to devote myself full time to writing. I also suspected that if I didn't do it now—that is, at the end of the current school year—I probably never would. I felt that no matter how successful my teaching career was, I would consider myself a failure.

By spring, Suzanne and I had discussed and analyzed the idea as fully as we could. We talked with Dale about it and also asked Jane and Michael's advice. They suggested I write about our experience of losing Peter. They pointed out that the subject of death and grieving was not a fully exhausted one in the book trade, and, as an unpublished writer in today's market, I would stand a better chance beginning with a work of nonfiction.

Around the time of spring vacation, I told Gardiner

my plans. I was both exhilarated and frightened at my decision. Emotionally and financially I had a lot riding on it. I was also haunted by the realization that if I were successful at what I had wanted for years to do, it would be as a result of Peter's death. That was a sweet irony to contemplate.

CHAPTER

13

IN THE LATE SPRING Peter's friend Coral stopped by. She told us that she'd heard recently that Peter had actually been found by a motorist on his way home. The man had checked for vital signs but found none. He'd tried to rouse a house or two, but could get no response. He'd then driven home and phoned the police.

This intelligence made it all the more important that we knew that Peter had been killed instantly. We felt that it would have been more than we could have borne to think that he had lain seriously injured on the side of the road and died from lack of prompt attention. As it was, Coral's news was terribly upsetting; it brought back all the old horror. A sudden surge of emotional and physical malaise swept over me as if I'd stepped on an electrified grating, for it ran through me like a current and was stunning in its intensity.

The feelings generated by Coral's news, however, made me realize that the passage of time had made a difference.

During the first few months I had wondered, almost obsessively, what his actual dying had been like. In the last second had he realized the mortal jeopardy he was in? Had he hit the pole screaming in terror?

I realized that I no longer worried about these questions, not because I'd told myself they were unanswerable, nor because I'd made a conscious decision to drop the matter. After hearing Coral's news and experiencing the old pain, I recognized that for some time I'd simply ceased to be bothered by the subject.

Perhaps this signified my acceptance of his death—probably *adjustment to* would be the better expression. He's dead and I know it, feel it, sense it, grasp it, acknowledge it. He's gone and he's not coming back. Seldom did the fact of his death sneak up on me unawares as it had in the early days. Seldom did I now shake my head as though trying to clear it or explode my breath in disbelieving shock when the fact of his death swept over me. Seldom was I any longer startled by the fact of his death. But I was now missing him more.

I understood that a subtle transition in the nature of my grieving had taken place: for some time I had been grieving more over his absence than over his death. In the beginning I had been so shocked at his death that missing him had been an irrelevant consideration. But it wasn't any longer. I was also conscious that most of the time now my pain was merely a dull ache. Most of the time.

Every now and then, though, I'd get a feeling of pain so sharp, so cutting, so unbearable that I would think I'd finally unraveled all the layers of pain that lay between the event and my grief. The pain was tangible, located in the center of my being. It would last only a moment, but it stunned me, took my breath away, left me exhausted.

As the end of the first year began to heave into sight, I found myself taking stock. I was acutely conscious of missing him, of grieving at what he had lost, but I was also aware of some benefits that had accrued, unpalatable as such an idea was. Sometimes I would think, *"Well, at least I don't have to listen to that music blaring"*; or *"I don't have those demands upon my time"*; or, *"Now I don't have to feel all that anxiety about him."* But then it would rush in what a small price these considerations were to pay for his existence, and the old guilt would again start its insidious work.

I could take some solace, however, from the fact that our relationship had been improving, my not wanting him to accompany me to Colorado notwithstanding. I recalled that it was about this time a year ago that he and I had had quite a session. It had been a Tuesday night, because Suzanne was in town at Dale's. Peter was not allowed out on school nights, but he'd given me some reason why he needed to go to Mark's. He'd said he would be home by eight, so I'd said all right. Around nine o'clock he called. I knew at once that he was drunk. He said he wanted to talk to with me about some things. I offered to get him, but he said Mark would drive him home.

When he got home, I saw that he had quite a package on. We sat in the living room. He trotted out his list of grievances and really tore into me. We must have talked for over an hour, but I only remember bits and snatches of the conversation, although I certainly recall the major themes.

He was agitated and emotional. I remember his saying,

"I wanna talk to you and I want you to fucking listen without any bullshit." He said he loved me and felt that I loved him, although I had a strange way of showing it at times. Why didn't I act more like I loved him? He was furious that I didn't treat him as an adult—or the near adult he was.

For my part, I mostly listened. I knew he was getting some important feelings out, and it didn't matter that he was swearing and yelling at me. After he'd started seeing Dale, we'd had a chat or two, and Peter was allowed to say anything to me so long as it was in the context of a discussion. Diction was unimportant—feelings and honesty mattered. Once, *not* during a discussion, we had begun to have words about something, and both of us had quickly grown angry. His language had been rough, and he'd suggested I perform coitus with myself and also called into question the legitimacy of my parentage. I'd gone for him and he'd been out the door like a shot. I'd known I stood no chance of catching him, so I'd settled for hurling a few epithets of my own after him. Another time he'd called me a "flabby old fart."

On this occasion, however, he could use whatever language he wanted. Although it hurt, I knew it was important that he vent his feelings. I realized, too, that for him to explode at me this way indicated that he cared for me. It was unmistakable that beneath the rage there was love. So even while he was calling me names and telling me what I was full of, I felt pretty good. Also, it was good to hear what he really thought of me. It wasn't as bad as it could have been—the negatives were balanced by the positives.

But there were some unpleasant negatives. One of them

was my temper. He reminded me of an incident years ago, when his friend Ricky had been up for the weekend. At one point Peter had said something rude and provocative to me, and I'd stormed up to him and given him a violent shove that put him on his butt. "I wanted to kill you, doing that in front of Ricky!" he cried.

"Sometimes I wish you would die," he said. Then the tears started again. "But I don't want you to die," he nearly wailed. "I love you. But when you do things like that, I feel so bad."

He covered a number of other points. The only one I remember was that I made him feel that his friends weren't welcome. I was surprised to hear that, but I quickly realized that there was undoubtedly a good deal of truth to it. I told him I would do something about that. I would also try harder to control my temper. I said how rotten I felt about chasing him out of the house that time, even though he'd been out of line.

At the close of our conversation, he said he knew he'd screwed up, but that was behind him. I told him I hoped in the future he wouldn't feel he needed to get drunk in order to talk with me. "You've said some hard things, kiddo, but they needed saying, and I'm okay."

I had him drink several glasses of water and take some aspirin. I knew from experience that they'd take the edge off his hangover. We hugged each other and he lurched off to bed.

I realized there was more to this guy than I'd recently been giving him credit for. I didn't expect a full turn-around, but I felt much better about his chances of pulling himself together. He'd shown a fair amount of self-awareness in some of his remarks, not to mention some uncomfortably accurate comments about me. I wondered how much of the fault was mine and how much was his. Was the problem within him, that he had to get drunk to level with me, or, for all my fine rhetoric, was the problem within me?

I still don't have an answer to that. I worry that too often I didn't help him but turned away, pretending I just didn't see.

On the Friday before Mother's Day, Suzanne arrived home from work looking shaken. "I saw Peter today," she said.

"That's a nice, provocative opening," I replied. "What the hell do you mean?"

"I saw a kid in Stamford who looked just like Peter, especially from the back—his hair, his build, the way he walked. He turned a corner, and I turned onto a street I wasn't going to use just to get a look at his face. I had to. It wasn't Peter, of course, but for those few moments it was shocking."

We talked about her experience, and Suzanne said she suspected that on some level she'd been looking for Peter, and that's why she'd *found* him. "Another form of denial, I suppose," she remarked.

We never celebrated synthetic commercial holidays like Mother's Day or Father's Day, but this incident, together with all the public emphasis on MOTHER, reminded me that another aspect of my grieving concerned Suzanne. I had a sense, at times exquisite, of her maternal suffering.

From the beginning I'd tried to imagine what special agony she had to be undergoing. If I was hurting as I was, what must she be experiencing? She, who had carried him inside her, who had brought him to birth and held him as an infant and dreamed the dreams that mothers dream, had to feel a lacerating pain that I could only guess at. How could she bear the fact that this extension of herself, yet a being of its own, had ceased to be?

I also found it painful to think of their relationship, which for many years had been truly good. Suzanne could be as short-tempered, inconsistent, and selfish as the next person, but there was a solid bond of love between them that no amount of familial wrangling could destroy. She could drive him nearly crazy on occasion with what he perceived to be her nagging and inconsistency, but from the time he was a baby she'd made him feel so loved and so wanted that he'd developed a sense of self-assurance and self-worth that could withstand the worst maternal bitchiness. As Peter got older they had some donnybrooks, but there was never any question of irreparable estrangement taking place.

Suzanne had responded better than I to Peter's teenage growing pains. Although she had often been frustrated and angered by his behavior and attitude, she had kept their lines of communication open. Consequently, he'd taken serious problems to her, which usually resulted in lengthy, intense conversations. Typically, he'd gone to Suzanne when he'd been having a problem with a girlfriend. He'd been terribly upset and told her he couldn't stand the mental anguish. She'd let him talk it out and made a few helpful suggestions. They'd both ended up in tears on that occasion.

In bad moments, I thought I'd go mad wondering how she could keep her sanity, how she could survive this loathsome ordeal. Whenever I witnessed her suffering, I felt shriveled by my helplessness, at my inability to cure her pain. I despaired at her despondency. At those times when we reached out to each other, which were often, I had a strong sense of togetherness, yet a sense of aloneness as well, for the death of a loved one brings home to us our essential isolation as does nothing else in the world.

Within a few months of Peter's death, Suzanne realized that her maternal instincts were still alive. She found the quiet, nearly empty house depressing. I didn't, and this led to some conflict between us. For most of the first year, I found it almost unbearably painful to have Peter's friends over. They were *his* friends, and it was unnatural for them to be at our house without Peter. They were too much a reminder of his absence. I dreaded their appearance, either singly or together, although with the passage of time and the chance to know them better, it ceased to be a burden.

As Suzanne pointed out to me when we discussed this problem, I had kids at school, some of whom were Peter's friends as well. But she had no one. This need, combined with her professional training and her psychoanalytical experience with Dale, led her to start a sibling group for teenagers who'd lost a brother or sister.

In part, this idea grew out of Compassionate Friends. Several of the bereaved parents in our group had teen-age children, and they often expressed concern about the effect of their children's deaths upon the surviving ones. There had been a sibling group for a brief time before we joined Compassionate Friends, but it hadn't worked well. Suzanne's group, however, was a success from the start, which didn't surprise me in the least. Unlike so many professionals, Suzanne didn't wear her professionalism on her sleeve. That is, she didn't toss jargon around—"What you're experiencing is the delayed shock syndrome"—or display that detached attitude which suggests a lack of personal interest or involvement. Nor did she imply condescension by talking down to them. She dealt openly and honestly with her own feelings, which quickly prompted them to respond in kind. The smallness of the group, usually six or seven, created an intimate atmosphere which also encouraged the kids to open up. Discussions often ranged far afield to encompass other problem areas, such as parents, school, and dating. The kids came from different towns, and, although none of them had known each other before, they soon developed a strong bond of mutual caring.

The sibling group and the fairly frequent visits by Peter's friends did a lot to assuage Suzanne's feelings of emptiness. But nothing, of course, could fill the void created by Peter's death. That was a gaping chasm that a lifetime of inspiring experiences couldn't fill. Nor could I. And that's been the central paradox in our relationship since Peter's death. There's an unbreakable bond, yet an unbridgeable gap between us.

As the school year drew to a close, I was in Gardiner's office one day when he told me that a small delegation of seniors was outside waiting to see me. They were going to present me with the yearbook. Normally, such presentations were done during prize-day ceremonies, but Gardiner said that this unusual procedure was being followed because the page opposite mine was a remembrance of Peter. Although they still intended to make a presentation on prize day, the seniors, after talking with

Gardiner, felt that under the circumstances it would be insensitive to spring it on me publicly.

When they handed me the yearbook, I opened it to the dedicatory page. Opposite was Peter's memorial page, bordered in black with a picture of him at the top and my poem underneath. I again experienced that sense of numbness, of deadness. I knew it was a gesture of affection on their part, both to me and to Peter. I could sense them looking intently at me, watching for my reaction, undoubtedly for my approval. I was so deeply touched that I couldn't cope with it emotionally. I hoped they would understand that the silence of their usually glib English teacher was a tribute to their generosity and thoughtfulness, a measure of my feeling for them. I thanked each one, shaking his hand.

The students at Stamford Catholic remembered Peter also. Although he'd only been there one year, they devoted two pages to him under the heading, "The Senior Class Remembers Peter Mitchell." One page had his picture and my poem. The other page, under a picture of a woodland scene with a stream running over rocks, had a quotation from Charlie Daniels's song "Reflections":

> Above all the rest
> I'll miss you the most
> And I loved you the best.
> I'll thank God I was blessed
> Just to know you.
>
> But it's all right now,
> Keep on singing loud,
> It's all right now,
> Heaven should be proud.

Peter had attended concerts of the Charlie Daniels Band a number of times. Suzanne said Peter would have been especially proud that the same words his friends applied to him at his death had originally been written to Ronnie Van Zant, the lead singer of another of his favorite groups, Lynyrd Skynyrd, at his death.

The end of the school year was difficult for me. I was acutely conscious that Peter should have been graduating. That thought added to the depression I normally experienced at that time of year. Since becoming senior adviser a few years before, I'd discovered that on an emotional level I felt deserted by each class as it graduated. The fact that a number of boys kept in touch was irrelevant—the class was leaving me. Added to that, this year I was leaving school; I was leaving colleagues and students who'd come to mean a great deal to me.

To add to the downbeat ending of the school year, one of my eleventh-grade students died from a brain tumor. As fate would have it, his name was also Peter. He was a lovely young man, intelligent, motivated, considerate, and concerned. Surgery had failed to relieve the problem and he'd been out of school most of the year. By late May complications had arisen, and the doctors informed his parents, Nancy and Tom, that the end was near.

Peter died on the night of the senior prom. Gardiner and I were chaperoning the dance when we received a call from Nancy. Peter's oldest brother, Andy, had graduated the year before. He had recently returned from Annapolis, and, attired in his dress whites, was at the prom with his date. Gardiner and I had to break the news to him.

Suzanne and I spent the next evening with Nancy and

Tom. Although they manifested some signs of shock, they seemed more tired and resigned than anything else. Since their Peter had been terminally ill, his death had not been a stunning surprise to them as our Peter's had been to us. Their shock had been experienced when the nature of his illness had been disclosed. In both cases, however, the sense of loss was just as great, the pain of grieving just as severe, and the need for support just as necessary. We found it painful sharing this grim experience with them, but the pain was mitigated by the knowledge that our presence and comments were helpful. In fact, we were already in the process of discovering that one of the rewarding aspects of Compassionate Friends was being able to help those who were newer at the experience of bereaved parenthood.

On the day of the funeral, we went first to the funeral home. It was difficult looking at this Peter in his coffin. Images from a similar scene ten months earlier kept superimposing themselves upon the present. For a while I was neither here nor back there, but in a psychological limbo of my own, a region of emotional oblivion. It wasn't much of a place to be, but at least it was safe.

As Nancy and Tom are Roman Catholics, they had a Requiem Mass said, at which her brother, a priest, co-officiated. The pallbearers had been selected from the faculty, Gardiner and I among them. Additionally, I read the well-known passage for I Corinthians which contains the lines, "O death, where is thy sting? O grave, where is thy victory?" These are very moving and comforting words, if you can accept the idea behind them. Not for the first time of late, I wished I could.

After our experience in Colorado, and more recently

with Dr. Mitchell, we weren't surprised to find the interment at the cemetery to be the worst part of the ceremony for us. It was as if the proceedings up to that point could have been a macabre charade of some sort, a dry run for the ultimate eventuality. But the grotesque reality of the gravesite allowed no such fantasies.

Suzanne and I were in a deep funk for several days after the funeral. Our pain was intensified by the knowledge that the anniversary of our Peter's death was close upon us. We realized that to feel pain is to release pain, much as though a valve were turned, jettisoning pressure. But that understanding was of little comfort in those moments of racking distress. It seemed as though our progression through the grieving process was a series of two-steps-forward, one-step-backward. It couldn't go on like this forever. It couldn't.

CHAPTER

14

WE HAD HEARD several people at Compassionate Friends
say, "One day you will discover that you have reached the
point where the death of your child is no longer the central fact of your everyday existence. It will no longer be
the prime motivator of your thoughts and actions. It will
be there, all right, but it will have moved from center
stage to the wings. It will continue to wield its influence,
but it will no longer hold your attention before all else."
On the anniversary of Peter's death, I recalled those
words. I could sense that time approaching, but I hadn't
gotten there yet. As the year progressed, I had found myself going for hours, sometimes nearly a whole day, without thinking of him, but those were rare occasions.

Suzanne and I spent Peter's anniversary together. We'd
been so conscious of its approach that the day itself was
no worse than we'd anticipated. I found it hard to believe
that an entire year had passed. In a sense, the intervening

period had been timeless. I realized it had taken us a long time to get here, but when I thought of that lump of time —a year—it seemed incredibly long.

We talked a lot about Peter and reflected on this time last year. We also talked about ourselves. We knew we hadn't gotten to the point where we accepted his death, but we could come to terms with it. Suzanne told me that just the week before she'd been lying in bed and looked across the hall to Peter's door. She'd realized that he would never come out that door again. "I suppose that's an adjustment of sorts," she said. She also reminded me of something we'd heard at one of our meetings: if you can come to terms with your grief for your child, you have probably come to terms with your own mortality.

I was astonished to discover that Peter's death had indeed forced me to face the fact of my own mortality. Over the years I'd certainly thought about my death, but on an emotional level, and I'd always backed off when the going got rough. In the course of my grieving over Peter, I had somehow allowed myself to *feel* my way through the idea of my death. I felt the same shock of horror and denial when contemplating my death that I'd experienced at Peter's. Before I realized it, I was grieving for myself as well as for Peter. His mortality had shown me the truth about my own with crushing impact. On his anniversary, then, I was amazed at feeling at ease about my own fate. I suppose I'd moved from simply acknowledging death toward an acceptance of it.

I believe Suzanne had moved in that direction as well. Several times over the past few months, she had said to me that she no longer feared her death. In fact, it could well have been her comments that started me moving in that direction. I couldn't get inside her head, of course, so I didn't know how deep or firm her acceptance was. But then I was none too sure about the depth or firmness of my own.

You either grow as a result of a death like Peter's, or you stagnate, because you'll never be the same again. I didn't know about myself, although I hoped I was more open and sensitive than before. I could see clearly, however, that Suzanne was in the process of growing. Her work with the sibling group alone was evidence of that. But even this achievement was a source of difficulty, for the characteristic of growth is considered a positive attribute, and you feel guilty that something positive could come as a result of your child's death.

We both recognized that we were still a long way from exorcising the evil spirits of guilt and rage within us. I was healthy enough to be able to be angry with Peter for dying, but not so healthy that I didn't feel guilty about feeling that way. And doubts remained as well. Sometimes I wondered if I were dwelling on his death too much—wallowing, so to speak—as though my suffering would make up to him for my shortcomings while he was alive. The most persuasive sense of guilt, however, came from this: I was still alive while he was dead.

I also understood that it would take more than a year to dissipate my anger over Peter's death. I suspected I had a reservoir which would supply me a lifetime. Just a few weeks before, I'd uncovered more dope paraphernalia of his while going through some junk in the garage, and I'd been swept with my old rage at him. At once I'd been swamped with guilt at feeling such a terrible emotion about my dead child. But then another wave of rage at him had broken over me, because his death prevented me from feeling angry without also feeling guilty. Around and around we go. Christ!

We found comfort, Suzanne especially, in remembering stories or anecdotes told us in the early days that revealed the nice side of Peter. The mother of one of his friends said Peter had stopped by one day, but her son hadn't been there. She'd been baking cookies, and Peter had sat with her in the kitchen, polishing off the cookies and chatting away. The Scandinavian family of another friend had adopted a Puerto Rican girl a few years younger than Peter and his friends. Apparently she was self-conscious about looking different and being younger. Most of the kids who stopped over ignored her, but Peter, we were told, always spoke to her. Greg's mother said she and Greg had stopped at Peter's gas station once, and Peter had made it a point to include her in the conversation and not just talk to Greg. Several kids said that wherever Peter was, the party was. I felt a bit ambivalent about that one. But the point is that these unimportant, common-place incidents were significant to us for what they said about Peter. Remembering those nice things people had said to us in the first week or so gave warmth and pleasure now.

We could also take pleasure in recalling incidents of our own concerning him. One such good memory had been brought to mind earlier in the month, because it had involved a paper sack full of fireworks which one of his aunts and uncles had brought him from Florida several years before. We hadn't made up our minds whether to let him have them. He'd asked if he could set off just one. We'd said okay. A few minutes later an explosion in the back yard rattled the windows. "What's the damn fool think he's doing?" I yelled at Suzanne as we headed for the door. "He'll have the cops on us."

As we were going out the door, I saw Peter turning the corner toward the back of the house himself. When we caught up with him, he was looking with amazement at a singed depression in the lawn. Bits of paper and cardboard were fluttering slowly back to earth. It appears he'd selected a rocket of some sort. He'd left the sack in the back and with uncharacteristic caution moved to the other side of the house before igniting the rocket. It had soared over the house and, with flames flowing behind, plunged unerringly into the sack. We all had a good laugh at the time.

That night we went to dinner with a Compassionate Friends couple with whom we'd become good friends. Claire and Bob had lost their three-year-old son, Blair, a year and a day before we'd lost Peter. We had an elegant and expensive dinner with them and their teenage son, Chris, who devoured everything in sight. It helped a lot to be with them because, as trite as it sounds, it does help to know you're not the only ones who hurt.

Over dinner, Bob told me about a man he'd met at a conference recently. The chap had lost his son several years ago. For the first three years of his bereavement, the man had been unable to cry, or talk, or otherwise find release for the tensions he was bottling up inside. One day he was about to toss some old, cracked china in the garbage, when he started throwing it against a large rock by his garage. It felt so good he went back to his house. got some more, and broke that too. As he was hurling it at the rock, he began to cry and could feel rage pouring out of him. Soon he started going to tag sales, buying all the cheap porcelain he could find. When he felt the need, he would take a stack and smash it against the rock. It had been remarkably therapeutic. He'd told Bob, "If you're ever in my area, drop by and we'll break a few plates."

"There are many different roads to recovery," Bob said to me, "but they all have one thing in common. Whether you talk, or write, as you're doing, or break china, you've got to get the crud out of your system. You can't just swallow your feelings; you've got to find release. I couldn't for my first year and it damn near wrecked me."

Suzanne and I sat up for a while before going to bed. I mentioned Bob's comment that you "had to get the crud out." I said I felt sure that we'd been doing that. Although we were still in the grip of anguish, we were aware of the curative power of time passing. We knew we had a long way to go but, using the year's passage as a bench mark, we understood that we'd come a fair distance. We'd gotten to the point where a new normality obtained. It had been a shock to realize that *normal* was not having our child, but we were now operating within that context. We were adjusting to living without Peter, but we sure as hell hadn't fully accepted that fact.

On this memorial night we wondered how we'd survived. We knew the support of our family and friends, the advice of people like Sally Bowers and Dale, and the help and companionship of Compassionate Friends had all contributed. Underlying those reasons, of course, was our resolve to deal with Peter's death as openly and directly as possible. Beyond that, I suppose some inner core had simply refused to surrender.

But it was still a son of a bitch. I thought back to that night a year ago by the side of the road, when my posterity lay broken at my feet, when our chance for immortality had been destroyed in one senseless, meaningless, random moment. Neither of us could answer the persistent, eternal question: *Why?*

Still, we had each other and that counted for a lot. I went to the kitchen to lock the back door and make sure Sir Benjamin had water. I went back into the living room and Suzanne took my hand.

"I love you," she said.

"Me too, Lovey," I answered.

We have suffered, but we have survived; we are hurting, but we are enduring.

I turned off the lights and we went upstairs to bed.

EPILOGUE

THE WRITING of this book was an ordeal. It proved more difficult and more painful than I'd anticipated. Several times I considered dropping the project, but the idea that this would be a memorial of sorts to Peter kept me at it.

I'm glad now I did. By the time the book was near completion, I had come to realize that writing it had been extraordinarily therapeutic. By putting into words in an organized fashion the events, thoughts, and feelings attendant upon his loss, I gained an emotional and intellectual understanding of what we'd gone through and where we'd arrived. The process of recovery is so slow, so fluctuating, and so visceral that it's extremely difficult to understand what is happening to you as it happens. By forcing myself to relive the events and reexperience the feelings of that first year, as well as reexamine the relationship the three of us had, I have found a degree of peace I would not have thought possible. That's not to say I'm over my grief, that pain and anger and guilt are strangers to me. I'm simply better able to cope with those nasty characters when they drop by.

It's impossible for us—I take the liberty of speaking for Suzanne here—to identify those points where our pain lessened appreciably, but they did occur. We hurt less now than we did. I believe we're stronger and better people than we were—more open, more caring, more sensitive and certainly in Suzanne's case, more helpful to others. That's the meaning, and the only meaning, I've been able to find in Peter's death. We could have remained passive and slowly drowned in our misery, but that would have been an insult to his memory, and indeed made his death meaningless. And it's not easy to find meaning in an event of this nature. You have to labor painstakingly at it, search diligently to find it. You have to drag meaning out of the experience.

Finally, the fact that our son's death was *not* dramatic, exceptional, or bizarre makes our trauma more accessible to others. Our tragedy was such a pedestrian affair that what we experienced might be beneficial to others to hear about, be they bereaved parents or not. There were none of those great melodramatic incidents so beloved by the writers of popular fiction. Nor are we celebrities who employ a ghost writer to inform a panting public how we laughed-on-the-outside-while-we-cried-on-the-inside. The ordinariness of our tragedy suggests that our story might be helpful to others.

If that's the case, perhaps we've found more meaning in Peter's death.